Breakthrough Community Change

Breakthrough Community Change

A Guide to Creating Common
Agendas That *Change Everything*

PAUL BORN

BK

Berrett–Koehler Publishers, Inc.

Berrett-Koehler Publishers, Inc.
1333 Broadway, Suite 1000
Oakland, CA 94612-1921
Tel: (510) 817-2277
Fax: (510) 817-2278
www.bkconnection.com

ORDERING INFORMATION
Quantity sales. Special discounts are available on quantity purchases by corporations, associations, and others. For details, contact the "Special Sales Department" at the Berrett-Koehler address above.
Individual sales. Berrett-Koehler publications are available through most bookstores. They can also be ordered directly from Berrett-Koehler: Tel: (800) 929-2929; Fax: (802) 864-7626; www.bkconnection.com.
Orders for college textbook / course adoption use. Please contact Berrett-Koehler: Tel: (800) 929-2929; Fax: (802) 864-7626.

Distributed to the U.S. trade and internationally by Penguin Random House Publisher Services.

Berrett-Koehler and the BK logo are registered trademarks of Berrett-Koehler Publishers, Inc.

Printed in Canada.

Berrett-Koehler books are printed on long-lasting acid-free paper. When it is available, we choose paper that has been manufactured by environmentally responsible processes. These may include using trees grown in sustainable forests, incorporating recycled paper, minimizing chlorine in bleaching, or recycling the energy produced at the paper mill.

Library of Congress Cataloging-in-Publication Data
Names: Born, Paul, author.
Title: Breakthrough community change : a guide to creating common agendas that change everything / Paul Born.
Description: First Edition. | Oakland, CA : Berrett-Koehler Publishers, [2023] | Includes bibliographical references and index.
Identifiers: LCCN 2022041889 (print) | LCCN 2022041890 (ebook) | ISBN 9781523002177 (paperback) | ISBN 9781523002184 (pdf) | ISBN 9781523002191 (epub) | ISBN 9781523002207
Subjects: LCSH: Community development. | Community organization.
Classification: LCC HN49.C6 B673 2023 (print) | LCC HN49.C6 (ebook) | DDC 307.1/406—dc23/eng/20220923
LC record available at https://lccn.loc.gov/2022041889
LC ebook record available at https://lccn.loc.gov/2022041890

First Edition
30 29 28 27 26 25 24 23   10 9 8 7 6 5 4 3 2 1

Book producer and text designer: Maureen Forys, Happenstance Type-O-Rama
Cover designer: Daniel Tesser
Copyeditor: Rachel Monaghan

To the Tamarack Community
A connected force for community change

Contents

**PART II: SKILL SETS FOR COMMUNITY
CHANGE**

    Community Change   129

12 ABCD: Asset-Based Community Development   137

13 Collective Impact   145

14 Community Engagement   153

15 Community Innovation   165

16 Collaborative Leadership   171

17 Evaluations That Support Community Change   181

    Conclusion: Be Careful What You Wish For   193

    Discussion Guide   197

    Notes   199

    With Thanks   203

    Index   205

    About the Author   215

Foreword

I HAVE BEEN WAITING FOR PAUL'S latest book, *Breakthrough Community Change*, for some time now. Before he started writing the book, I had asked Paul to host a private webinar for the stewards and faculty of the Asset-Based Community Development (ABCD) Institute, specifically to share the methodology he developed for large-scale community change. Paul's ideas are unique in that they have been tested in the "real world" and have had a dramatic impact, measurably improving communities throughout Canada, the United States, and around the world.

Paul's work has improved the lives of thousands of people. The ideas and methodology that he perfected during his time at the Tamarack Institute have ended poverty for many people, given hope to young people for better futures, helped cities prepare for climate change, and deepened the experience of community, which in turn has reinforced citizenship in entire neighborhoods.

Paul has been a faculty member (now known as a steward) of the ABCD Institute for several decades. The ABCD Institute is at the center of a large and growing global movement that considers local assets as the primary building blocks of sustainable community development. Building on the skills of local residents, the power of local associations, and the supportive functions of local institutions, asset-based community development draws upon existing community strengths to build stronger, more sustainable communities for the future. Paul and the Tamarack Institute, which he cofounded with philanthropist and business leader Alan Broadbent, have provided significant leadership in advancing the work of ABCD in Canada and beyond.

In this book Paul provides practical and easy-to-follow steps that anyone can replicate to improve their neighborhoods and communities. He also provides exercises that can help citizens to collectively challenge their mental models and to work with people across sectors, embracing differences and recognizing diversity as an asset to celebrate as essential to creating solutions to some of the most pressing problems facing our communities.

If you want to live in a better neighborhood, community, or city, read this book. If you fear the future and need hope that large-scale positive change is possible, read this book. If you are leading change in your community, I highly recommend using this book as a guide to improve your outcomes.

I listen to Paul Born when I want to know how people get together for the common good. He is a master practitioner and storyteller. If you want to know what lies beyond the radical individualism and collective incompetence that plague our modern lives, read this book.

—*John McKnight*

John McKnight is cofounder of the Asset-Based Community Development Institute and a senior associate of the Kettering Foundation. He is the author of *Associational Life* (Kettering Foundation Press, 2022) and *The Careless Society* (Basic Books, 1996) and coauthor of *The Connected Community* (Berrett-Koehler, 2022), *Building Communities from the Inside Out* (ACTA, 1993), *The Abundant Community* (Berrett-Koehler, 2010), and *An Other Kingdom* (Wiley, 2015).

Introduction

Whole Community Change

OUR WORLD IS FACING PRESSING and relentless problems. Climate change, poverty, disease, racism, and inequality are jeopardizing the lives and well-being of all citizens. We need meaningful breakthroughs to create large-scale, community-wide change. Incremental change will not provide the momentum needed to tackle these unyielding challenges. It is most important for us to work as a united force to innovate, cooperate, and collaborate if we are to achieve the breakthroughs needed to redress and make significant progress to improve the quality of life for all.

Cities, towns, municipalities, neighborhoods, and communities are in a unique position to prioritize innovative approaches to achieve large-scale impact through breakthrough community change. These groups can act at a manageable scale to collaborate at a magnitude that can result in noteworthy changes within a defined geographic area. They can maximize breakthrough community change approaches to transform the root causes of social problems in their communities. As business, government, nonprofits, and people with lived/living experience gather to network and learn from each other, new and creative ideas emerge and the momentum for change is fueled. This intense collaboration results in some of the most profound social changes, including ending poverty, reducing cancer rates, and becoming carbon neutral. In the end, the community is a better and more vibrant place for all.

Breakthrough community change recognizes that we can do more together when we unite than any of us can do alone. By working toward a common agenda and with a common approach, we bring the unique skills and assets of each individual into the process of change. When we become an interconnected force, large-scale breakthrough community change is possible.

I believe that many of the social issues and the brokenness we see and feel in our communities are felt by most of us. We see many different people struggle, including single parents, alienated families, young people, and many dealing with mental health issues. We see the effects of climate change, poverty, and racism on our neighbors. We are somehow frozen—frozen together like ice cubes that melted just enough to touch each other before they froze again. We want to act, but we are stuck. Or maybe we are just waiting for a sign or an opportunity to act. And yet, so often we wait, and nothing changes.

The world needs our discontent with the ways things are. If we were content, we would accept the brokenness we see daily in our communities. We would accept the fear our children have of their future and climate change. We would accept the misery of the homeless mother struggling to care for her children, and the fractious and seemingly futile struggle of people faced with racism and the inequity it breeds. We would accept the hunger pangs that are never satisfied, the workers that earn less than they need. Our discontent leads us and the organizations we work within to seek breakthroughs.

Many of us have experienced breakthroughs that have changed our lives. We have had flashes of pure clarity and "aha" moments that seem to transform old ways of thinking, reinvigorate energies, and lead us to a new, more innovative way of living. Throughout this book, you will read stories about the breakthroughs of many individuals I have coached and mentored along their journey to engage an entire community in creating a large-scale impact. The stories I share will illustrate how the power of personal and organizational breakthroughs can be harnessed at the community level to increase engagement, identify assets, and work collaboratively to build a common agenda and work toward whole community change.

Many of us have been part of a team or group working in a community that has experienced a breakthrough. Community teams or groups usually have common goals and strive to work together to achieve an agreed-upon outcome. The best teams know how to engage creatively, challenge mindsets, and discover innovative ways of working together. This is the journey toward a community breakthrough.

Breakthrough Community Change: A Guide to Creating Common Agendas That Change Everything illustrates the process of communities collaborating to achieve large-scale change and makes the approaches, ideas, techniques, and skills available to a growing field of changemakers. This book presents a practical approach that can inspire community leaders and social service providers to consider solving the root causes of problems rather than simply addressing their symptoms or alleviating their effects.

Part I of this book will lead you through a process of identifying your community's readiness for change: forming Leadership, Action, and Work Teams; creating a common agenda; and establishing plans for community engagement, internal and external communication, shared measurement, and governance. These efforts lead to the implementation of a community campaign that can result in large-scale community change.

Part I provides a road map to breakthrough community change. Essential to this journey is a common agenda. A common agenda is a result of building trust in new ways and forging a shared community commitment to the needed change. When people are committed to change, they bring forth individual and organizational assets that contribute to collective action. The process of developing a common agenda results in people being engaged, curious, and innovative. New creativity can be unleashed as people release old mental models and embrace collective ones. The process of building a common agenda unites a community and increases bonding across multiple sectors. A common agenda is the door that opens to breakthrough community change.

Critical to the journey toward impact is asking broader questions and measuring and observing interventions and effects for the change we want to see. Listening to people with lived experience, learning quickly, and adapting are critical to moving toward a strong impact. Progress should be tracked using a contribution mindset, rather than an attribution measurement approach. The evaluation process should be designed and carried out in ways that empower stakeholders and are organized around their questions.

Part II of this book provides more detailed descriptions of the approaches and skill sets (ideas and strategies) that can help you to develop the muscles needed to do the work described in Part I. The most effective community change-makers have an evolving awareness or knowledge of theories and concepts around how communities function, how policies are developed, and how people are engaged in the process of change. Most importantly, they are interested in how communities collaborate and authentically work together to achieve better outcomes. Effective community collaboration is complex and draws from the study of collective impact, asset-based community development, community engagement, social innovation, collaborative leadership, and participatory evaluation.

As founder and former CEO of the Tamarack Institute, I have worked with hundreds of communities as they worked through this process and made significant impacts on their community. One community I coached of over one hundred thousand people reduced decades of deeply entrenched poverty from 28 percent of the population down to 12 percent. I have seen the ideas shared in this book contribute tremendously to large-scale change in communities. These changes transform the root causes of social problems and result in large-scale, population-level impact. To achieve a population-level impact, we must recognize that the issues facing the community are radically interconnected. The deeper we understand and experience connections between each other and within the community, the more we will be able to uncover hidden resources and innovative ideas. When we unite within a network of committed individuals and agree on a common agenda for change, we move closer to comprehensive transformation and resolution of social and economic challenges.

The goal of the Tamarack Institute is to better understand community change and make the work of community change leaders easier and more effective. The Institute works in Canada, the United States, and worldwide to advance communities collaborating for population-level change. The Institute's forty-two thousand active learners are leaders in the processes of large-scale community change. This book is about sharing what we learned along the way and making the knowledge, processes, and strategies more accessible to a broader audience.

This journey started when my colleagues and I launched Opportunities 2000, a four-year campaign in the Waterloo Region of Canada with the goal of reducing poverty in our community to the lowest level in the country by the year 2000. As the work intensified and positive changes were realized and supported by strong outcome data, word spread quickly. By 2022 nearly five hundred communities in Canada and the United States joined together as a learning community called Vibrant Communities. These communities create common agendas and use the breakthrough community change ideas and practices described in this book to end poverty, secure youth futures, support climate transition, and deepen a sense of community. With more than 1 million people out of poverty, almost all the communities in the Vibrant Communities network have seen significant drops in poverty at the population level and improvements in the quality of life for all residents. Canada has reduced poverty dramatically. The 2000 poverty rate in Canada was 16.2 percent. Since the creation of Vibrant Communities, Statistics Canada reports the poverty rate has dropped to 6.4 percent in 2020, the lowest level of poverty in Canada's history.[1]

Collaborative community change is fueling worldwide change. Tamarack's Vibrant Communities uses the collaborative ideas and practices of breakthrough community change shared in this book with multiple campaigns in Canada, the Unites States, and around the world. Communities Building Youth Futures is using the strategies to identify their goal of improving high school graduation rates and youth engagement. Community Climate Transitions has taken on the task of combating climate change. Cities Deepening Community uses these strategies to strengthen citizenship and advance neighborliness. More examples of the effectiveness of the integration of multiple ideas on community change are described throughout the book.

Like you, when I read the newspaper or scroll through social media, I am struck by how many reports detail significant problems in my neighborhood, country, and around the world. At times I feel like I am being bombarded with such massive and complex problems that I am paralyzed with despair. As a community organizer for many years, I know well how easy it is to be overwhelmed by issues of recession, poverty, loneliness, youth mental illness, climate crises, rising rates of disease, and so many other social problems. Yet I know that I cannot be still. I cannot be silent. I must use my knowledge, experience, and energies to champion changes that will build better, stronger, and healthier lives for people in our communities around the world.

PART I
Communities Collaborating

THIS BOOK IS WRITTEN AS a guide for you to learn about building collaborative community change. The only right way to bring about change in your community is to find the way that works within your community's unique set of circumstances. I have found that once people get the idea of communities collaborating, they long to hear how other community leaders have done the work of large-scale change and use this information to fine-tune their own methodology.

It is important to declare my bias and the bias of the Tamarack Institute when describing "our kind" of communities collaborating work. As a coach, I perceive and work with communities through a collective impact lens. I have used the ideas and practices of collective impact because I believe that it is the most advanced form of communities collaborating. Rather than simply collaborating to improve how organizations in communities work together, collective impact calls us to seek large-scale, population-level impacts. This has been important to the campaigns Tamarack has supported. If you are unfamiliar with collective impact, Chapter 13 provides you with a summary of this methodology.

Even though I have a collective impact bias, I also share the ideas of many thought leaders and approaches. This book seeks to more generally consider approaches to communities collaborating, with only one of the approaches being collective impact.

My approach has been influenced by people that I consider mentors. Margaret Wheatley was my earliest influence when she released *Leadership and the New Science*. This book introduced me to systems change thinking and helped me see how community issues are integrated. I was also attracted to considering "simpler ways" of organizing groups of people, as Wheatley described so beautifully in her book *A Simpler Way*.

David Chrislip is a pioneer in the work of collaborative leadership. His books *Collaborative Leadership: How Citizens and Civic Leaders Can Make a Difference* and *The Collaborative Leadership Fieldbook* transformed how I understand leadership. Chrislip is interested in the attributes and the skill sets of collaborative leaders. His work inspired me to believe that collaborative community change could be taught and learned. I now understand how collaborative leadership is distinct from leadership development training.

Anne Kubisch was the director of the Aspen Institute's Roundtable on Community Change, which supports community development in disadvantaged communities. She published the Roundtable series *Voices from the Field I, II, and III*, which provides a comprehensive state-of-the-field analysis of community change initiatives. The Roundtable pioneered work in evaluating community initiatives and was integral in advancing the theory of change approach to planning. They pioneered work on structural racism. In many ways far ahead of her time, Anne and her team influenced how we understand outcomes and provide practical approaches for communities collaborating to create systemic change.

The White House Council for Community Solutions, initiated by First Lady Michelle Obama and President Barack Obama with support from Melody Barnes (assistant to President Obama and director of the Domestic Policy Council), was mandated to identify key attributes of effective community-developed solutions to our national problems. As part of this effort, the Domestic Policy Council worked to build capacity within communities to establish collaboratives for creating broad-based change. My interest was piqued when the Council released the *Community Collaborative Toolbox*. Later the Council came out to endorse collective impact, a process for community change most significantly advanced by Jenifer Splansky Juster, John Kania, Mark Kramer, and their colleagues at FSG. Melody Barnes left the White House to support the advancement of collective impact through the Aspen Institute's Forum for Community Solutions and to start the Opportunity Youth Forum. This work convinced me that the work of communities collaborating was entering a sort of golden age. Many more communities want to expand their knowledge and understanding of this approach to social change.

The Tamarack Institute has been the proving ground for many of the approaches described in this book. My thinking and work have been significantly influenced by long-time colleagues Liz Weaver and Mark Cabaj. Lisa Attygalle, Sylvia Cheuy, Alison Homer, Heather Keam, Laura Schnurr, Nathalie Blanchet, and Myriam Berube are noteworthy colleagues who have contributed to and expanded my thinking on community change. I share these names because the field surrounding communities collaborating is growing. There are many thought leaders in this space. Although I am sharing "my way," so many parts of the approach I am sharing represent "our way" of teaching community change at Tamarack. To learn more and to receive many practical tools, go to *TamarackCommunity.ca*.

1

Breakthrough Community Change

But we know for sure that these are days when the improbable can become the inevitable.

—JIM DWYER, *NEW YORK TIMES*, OCTOBER 25, 2014

A GUIDE TO:

- Rethinking your motivation to help
- Embracing "root problem" solutions
- Moving from incremental to large-scale change

I SENSE THAT YOU ARE READING this book because you want more for your community. Like me, you realize that even though there is so much amazing work being done, by such amazing and dedicated people, "the problems" just seem to be getting worse. You hope that we might solve the issues that are causing people to suffer. You want real change.

You are looking for a breakthrough!

Breakthrough community change is recognizing that we can do more together when we unite our community than any of us can do individually. By working toward a common agenda and with a common approach, we bring the unique skills and assets of each individual into the process of change. When we become an interconnected force, large-scale break-through community change is possible.

I came to community work because I wanted to help people. My instinct is to just jump in and help. I help as a caring citizen, whether it is holding open a door, cooking at a soup kitchen, organizing my neighborhood's parties, or supporting a friend going through a health crisis. I help people as a professional counselor, job trainer, administrator, community organizer, and small-business coach.

I want to share a favorite childhood story of mine that describes my earliest motivation for helping others:

> The shore was littered with thousands of starfish that had washed up. A young boy was standing near the water, throwing them back into the ocean. A passerby approached the boy and asked, "Why are you throwing the starfish back into the sea? Do you not realize that this is futile?" The boy reached down and picked up another starfish, threw it into the water, and said, "At least I helped this one."

I was inspired by the resilience of that little boy. I identified with him. His answers motivated me to keep working to help people despite the seemingly overwhelming problems that were rarely resolved. I did not question the boy's answer about helping just one.

I will never lose my instinct to help even just one person. I have, though, come to realize that to truly help people in need we must create the conditions to address the root problem they face.

My mentor and thesis advisor, Joe Schaeffer, shared his wisdom with me when I told him of my desire to end poverty in my community. He said, "If you want to end poverty you should ask those who care, and possibly those who do not, these questions: 'How might we create a community in which poverty could not exist? How then would we live within and with each other?'"

His response had a profound effect on me. It solidified my thinking, changed my understanding, and fueled my desire to address the root cause of poverty. My focus shifted from wanting to alleviate poverty to ending poverty—in other words, to shift the work from simply helping the poor live better lives to creating systems that would end poverty.

Today, if I were that boy standing on the beach confronting this overwhelming problem, the first thing I would do is run to the nearest village and organize the villagers to join me in working together to save as many starfish as we could. Once everyone was well organized and committed to saving the starfish that had washed up on the shore, I would host community conversations that would consider why all these starfish were stranded. I would seek the wisdom of the helpers. We would form an action team, climb into a boat, paddle out to sea, and try to find the source of the problem. Once we better understood what was going on, we would develop a plan to save the starfish. Then we would mobilize the community to enact the plan. With this united agenda, we would work together to achieve a collective impact, mobilizing the whole community and saving as many starfish as possible.

My Breakthrough

I have always trusted community. As a young boy, I grew up in a community of refugees who survived the terrible traumas of war and famine in their homeland of Ukraine. Both of my grandfathers had been executed during the purge of Stalin. As a family and a community of refugees, we survived and then thrived through what I like to call "a hive mind," where we worked and learned together. We made sense of the world together through our collective intelligence. Almost no one was unemployed in our community. If you lost your job, it was our community that helped make connections for you to find a new one. When we wanted to expand our farms, we talked to our neighbors. One neighbor learned how to grow raspberries, and soon we all grew them. Visiting after church services was as much a peer-to-peer business conversation as it was a social one. It was common to hear conversations where advice was readily shared. One neighbor would ask, "How did you say you prepared the raspberries for winter?" and others would chime in with their ideas. We were an interconnected community. We worked together utilizing this hive mind to improve outcomes. These early experiences shaped my approach to community change.

Many years later, I was standing at the lectern nervously shuffling my papers and waiting for the applause to subside. Nicholas You, then senior policy and planning advisor at UN-Habitat, had arrived in Waterloo, Canada, from Nairobi. He was here to give the Community Opportunities Development Association (CODA) a United Nations Habitat for Best Practice (Top 40) award for our work with poverty reduction in the Waterloo Region of Canada. As executive director of CODA, I was accepting the award. I should have felt proud, but instead I felt conflicted. There were hundreds of people in the room waiting to be inspired by my remarks. All I could think was, *Do we deserve this recognition?*

My remarks began with the standard thank-yous to the dignitaries in the room, the staff and volunteers who had worked so hard, and the partner organizations that had supported our success. I went on to share about the remarkable team that supported more than five thousand individuals and families to improve their economic security and raise themselves out of poverty. Our team supported people getting back to work, starting small businesses, and finding work after being displaced because of numerous factory closures. We helped thousands of families with children living in poverty by providing books for birthdays and hosting an annual Christmas party.

Our results were outstanding. Nearly 82 percent of the business start-ups we supported were still active after five years. The plant closure team successfully placed more than 90 percent of all the workers who had been displaced into new jobs. We had created a total community response to the problem of unemployment. United Nations Habitat wanted to spread the word about our work by giving us the award.

I had opened my speech the way most had expected, but then I paused. Through an uncomfortable silence, I looked up from my notes and surveyed our supporters in the audience. I closed my notepad, drank some water, and slowly began to speak.

"I find it interesting that we are being honored today," I said. "Of course, I am proud of the work we have done and the successes I have shared with you, but I am also perplexed, or maybe a better word is confused. You see, I get it that our outcomes are remarkable when compared to everyone else doing similar work in our community and beyond. I also understand that we have created a unique approach to helping unemployed people, and this should be recognized. But here is my dilemma. Even after all the success we accomplished over the past ten years, poverty has increased by nearly 5 percent in our community. That means things are getting worse for unemployed people. Things have gotten worse in our community and not better. I sense that when poverty increases in a community it is like a business losing shareholder wealth. When you lose significant shareholder wealth you get fired,

not recognized. So, you see, I do not think we should accept
this award today."

As you can imagine, these comments did not go over so
well with the audience. Nicholas You got up after me and
shared with the audience that we were being recognized not
only for our remarkable work but also for creating what he
called a "human problem-solving machine." He went on to say
that the broader outcomes, such as our unemployment rate,
were subject to so many outside influences that are beyond
our control. The audience agreed with him, and despite my
"moment of confusion," we received our award.

My struggle with accepting the award was well founded.
Mark Cabaj, a promising student at the time, had approached
me to host an internship for him. I was immediately taken
by his sharp mind and discontent with the current state of
communities in Canada. He had just returned from working
in Europe, where he supported businesses and social development and witnessed the fall of the Berlin Wall. Mark had
grown up on a small farm in rural Alberta. He has become
one of the foremost experts in the field of development evaluation and is called on around the world for his knowledge of
community change.

Mark convinced me that CODA should do a cost-benefit
analysis and consider the opportunity costs of the work we
were doing to determine where we should invest our energy
and money to achieve the greatest impact. We brought together
some of the best and brightest people and community leaders
to form an advisory council. Members of the advisory council included Mike Lewis of the New Economy Development
Group, Robin Murray from the London School of Economics,
and other local community leaders. The goal of the advisory
council was to provide feedback on the work of our organization and give insight into our work going forward. They

concluded that even though CODA ran exceptional programs, its real benefit was that it had created new ways of working together as a community. They emphasized that we created a systems change approach to our work.

The advisory council highlighted that all of CODA's services addressed the needs of individuals through transactional engagements and simultaneously sought to address a larger community problem by drawing on the existing assets of the community. The advisory council felt we had a remarkable ability to turn everything we did into a campaign. We organized a whole community response by uniting people in collective action toward a common outcome. We went beyond helping people to live better lives; we wanted to solve the systemic problems they were facing. The answer to almost every problem we faced was mobilizing our community. This was a powerful insight into our cost-benefit as an organization.

The advisory council helped us to identify and understand that we were working in a new way, even if we had not done so intentionally. This understanding and the United Nations award experience helped us to formulate an innovative understanding of not only the problem of poverty but the solutions required to end it. It was our breakthrough moment.

Within six months of the award ceremony, I had raised over $1 million from business leaders and private foundations. With Mark Cabaj, we launched Opportunities 2000, a four-year millennium campaign with the goal of reducing poverty in our community to the lowest level in Canada. It was a campaign that was to become our community's gift to the world and our way of celebrating the new millennium.

Essentially, we had two complementary ideas. First, if we were going to significantly reduce poverty in our community, the whole community would need to change, just a little bit.

We asked, "What would less poverty look like if we all just changed 10 percent?"

The second idea was that we would act as a United Way fundraising campaign on steroids. We would run our campaign for four years. United Way brought leaders in business, labor, community, and government together with everyday citizens to work in a united, nonpartisan way, and to raise money for needy agencies that were making their communities great places for everyone to live. We wanted to operate in a similar fashion, uniting all sectors, developing a plan to reduce poverty, and working together to make it happen.

We believed that if we were to end poverty, we would need to change our whole community's approach to poverty reduction. This would require us to build new thinking systems, establish new relationships, and work together toward a collective impact—plus, hope for a few miracles along the way.

Our breakthrough community change began.

2

Preparing for the Journey

*Our experience is that it's unusual for organizations
running programs to think about the whole population, and whole community change, and often people
don't believe that change at that scale is possible.*

—BILL CRIM, UNITED WAY SALT LAKE CITY

A GUIDE TO:

- Understanding the importance of your personal
  readiness

- Affirming your need to expand your understanding of
  community change ideas

- Starting on the four paths for the learning journey

JUST ABOUT EVERY WEEK WE read about another
serious problem facing our community. We are frus-
trated as poverty increases and angry as racism hurts our
neighbors. We feel helpless as our young people face increas-
ing mental health stress. People in our communities are looking for ways to create a better world. Yet it seems we are just
growing further apart.

We need to look for more effective ways of tackling what
seem to be stubborn and intransigent community problems.

Recognizing the importance of engaging citizens in decisions that affect their lives is an essential step to large-scale community change.

By strategically uniting community assets—what is strong in a community—around a common agenda, leaders create the conditions for a breakthrough that heals the brokenness in their communities. Fortunately, we can use our skills in community engagement, collaborative leadership, and social innovation to do just that.

Breakthrough community change happens when people want better outcomes and work together in their community. They learn about community engagement, bring community leaders together, create a common agenda, and work together to implement a campaign and achieve a collective outcome.

Breakthrough community change happens when diverse individuals from business, human service organizations, and government talk to each other and then reach out to individuals with lived/living experiences of the challenges a community seeks to overcome. By identifying community assets and fully engaging the whole community, everyone realizes how powerful they can be together.

Breakthrough community change seeks to harness the collective wisdom and intelligence of a community. When we embark on a journey to large-scale change, we develop new skill sets in collective impact, community engagement, collaborative leadership, asset-based community development, evaluation, and social innovation. Armed with this new knowledge, we are more prepared to help people in our community to envision and achieve better outcomes.

Breakthrough community change is about changemakers.

I want to share some stories that illustrate how communities realized a breakthrough. These are people I coached who sought better outcomes and were willing to adopt new ways of thinking and doing. These leaders created the conditions for a breakthrough that would heal the brokenness in their communities by strategically uniting community strengths around a common agenda. They honed their skills in collective impact, community engagement, collaborative leadership, asset-based community development, evaluation, and social innovation to move the community from talking to action to impact.

Elisabeth Buck is a changemaker. As director of Central Iowa's United Way, she supported numerous programs to improve the economic security of area residents by reducing barriers to opportunities. But it seemed the harder her team worked, the worse things got, especially for people of color and new immigrants. She wanted breakthrough community change. She united her community around a common agenda called Opportunities Central Iowa, and within three years they changed their whole community and supported twenty-five thousand Iowans to improve their economic security. Opportunities Central Iowa is evidence that communities collaborating for change can achieve breakthrough impacts.

Aysha Sheikh is a changemaker. She worked with an amazing team at the Maine Cancer Foundation to address growing cancer rates in the state. The new programs and research showed promise, but cancer rates climbed steadily. At the time, Maine had one of the highest cancer rates in the United States. Aysha wanted breakthrough community change. In 2016, Aysha and the Maine Cancer Foundation formed the Impact Cancer Network, uniting cancer survivors, medical professionals, legislators, and business leaders in Maine around a common agenda to reduce the incidence of cancer and mortality due to cancer. They changed their mandate from investing in research to investing in communities.

By 2018, they had completed their community plan, which led to a comprehensive Maine Cancer Plan 2021–2025.[1] Uniting their community with a common agenda changed everything.

Lyse Brunett is a changemaker. She observed the decline of the Saint Michel neighborhood in Montreal. This once-thriving neighborhood now had higher poverty and worse health outcomes than any other neighborhood in Montreal. Lyse wanted breakthrough community change. Lyse organized Saint Michel, mobilized key community leaders, united them to develop a common agenda for the community, and formed Vivre Saint Michel. Over the next twenty years, they turned the community around using a breakthrough community change approach and had amazing results. As of 2022 more than thirty-two neighborhoods in Montreal have reduced school dropout rates, increased health care for families, and implemented a street outreach program for youth.

Bill Gale was a changemaker. A retired banker, Bill met a homeless person in Saint John, New Brunswick. Bill invited the man to lunch. After hearing his story, Bill was moved to do more for his community. He invited his business leader friends to form the Business Community Anti-Poverty Initiative to help those living in poverty. Bill wanted breakthrough community change. He united business, community, and government leaders to launch Vibrant Saint John, which effectively reduced poverty from 27 percent in 1997 to less than 14 percent in 2016.[2] Bill and his team used a breakthrough community change approach to fundamentally transform their community.

These changemakers each transformed the way they thought about community change. Each embarked on a personal change journey. Each embarked on a learning journey. Each made a significant impact on his or her community.

Their change journey is in many ways similar to Marcy's.

Marcy's Learning Journey

I first met Marcy when she attended our five-day Communities Collaborating workshop. Marcy was ever positive, but tired. She was tired of partnering with community agencies and putting in huge amounts of work, only to see that nothing changed. Marcy's interest was piqued when she participated in my workshop Collective Impact—The First 12 Months. She began to imagine how she and her community could engage people with lived experiences. Her energy for the work was returning. She was on the verge of a personal breakthrough experience.

Marcy is an amazing community developer from a small city in Alberta, Canada. A social worker by training, she has done multiple jobs throughout her twenty-year career. At the time we met, she was an upper-mid-level city government manager and active in her provincial community developers' association. She had long desired a better quality of life for low-income citizens, worked to end homelessness, and provided improved housing for Aboriginal people and new Canadians in her community. Marcy was increasingly concerned that no matter how many great programs her city provided, the population-level statistics for vulnerable people did not seem to improve.

Over the next several years, Marcy participated in webinars and communities of practice and attended multiday workshops on community engagement and impact evaluation. She learned about collective impact and asset-based community development. She engaged community partners, low-income citizens, and business leaders in the learning journey. She was setting up the conditions for breakthrough community change in her community.

Two years after I first met Marcy, she shared what she had learned and how her community had changed. She acknowledged that she started out looking for a simple understanding that would build more effective collaborative action in her community. Collective impact was simple to explain. This fresh approach to community change excited others in her community. She quickly realized that for her community to make lasting change, they needed to get better at bringing the whole community into this work, including people with lived/living experiences and the business community. Asset-based community development and community engagement became critical to their work. These approaches provided a new commitment to involving everyone. When the community partners started using outcome tracking and sharing real data, Marcy began to understand the purpose of shared measurement. As the community partners began agreeing on key measures, Marcy's understanding of leadership shifted and her understanding of the community's role in collaborative change broadened. She was gaining clarity.

Marcy's story illustrates the process of breakthrough community change. Working toward a breakthrough community change challenges your mental models and fuels a desire to find more ways of getting to know your community. You can discover a community change idea that makes more sense than the way you are currently working. The idea energizes you. Like Marcy, you are preparing to develop the conditions necessary for breakthrough community change.

Four Paths to Follow

Both personal and community learning journeys are necessary for change. Everyone who seeks to expand their understanding of breakthrough community change begins from their personal reference point. You may be focused on the issues and want to learn all you can about them, such as how they emerge over time and what has been done to mediate them. You may be process-oriented and want to learn more about organizing and the actions of large-scale change. You may approach this work from a spiritual point and want to learn about finding the inner strength required to sustain a long and difficult journey to community change. Wherever you find yourself, start learning and be surprised by the discoveries you make along the way.

I suggest four paths that you may want to follow on your learning journey.

Learn Together

The first thing most people do when they embark on something new is to talk to others about it. The response from friends is critical to validating an idea and approach. I recommend forming a learning circle with a small group of people who also are looking for new ways forward and a whole community approach. You might start a learning circle with people inside your organization, or you might reach out to leaders you trust in the partner agencies. Forming a book club can be a good start. You can meet with like-minded people, read various books, and discuss them. The idea here is that you want to begin expanding your knowledge about how community change happens, how to agree on a common agenda and develop an openness to others' ideas. Once you can explain to others how a common agenda effects community change, you can broaden your circle. Often people will reach out to community leaders and hold dialogues that explore ideas like collective impact and discuss the preconditions for success. You might want to consider the list of resources at the end of each chapter in Part II to learn more.

Challenge Your Mental Models

A mental model is a description of your thinking system. When we explore our mental models, we can often expose personal biases that have been directing our lives for years. Mental models help to explain how we "see" the world. They evolve throughout our lifetimes and are frequently difficult to change. They are formed by our experiences, education, family history, and culture. Our mental model about how communities change comes from our experiences and education. You may be influenced by your parents' involvement in your community or by how your faith community emphasized service as imperative to faithfulness. You may have grown up giving food to the food bank or donating to the local homeless shelter. Our understanding of community change is often highly influenced by our informal and formal education. Taking time to understand your mental model of community is important in your journey.

Early in my career, as I was explaining the idea of community change to a colleague, he dismissed my idea and said, "I believe the only real change happens when we help someone to change through therapy." He was not interested in talking about the conditions that cause problems for people. He felt that only individuals could be healed, not systems or communities of people. "Communities are only healthy because the people in them are healthy," he said. I was shocked by how forcefully he made this claim. His mental model was entrenched, and it prevented him from seeing the potential for a better world. At the time I did not know how to engage him to consider a broader view.

My first book, *Community Conversations*, describes what I learned about whole community change. In observing how communities engage, I was struck by the power of group dialogue to gently challenge mental models. I found that when people heard each other's stories, they began to accept different ways of thinking about the problem. As I observed group dialogues over time, I found that communities could unthink, unlearn, and let go of their mental models long enough to engage in ideas about systems and whole community change thinking.

When exploring a new community change approach, I find it very helpful to start a journal. I keep notes about what I am learning and describe discoveries about my mental models. I love creating mind maps that allow me to brainstorm new ideas. Most of all, I love to write about the questions that are arising for me along my learning journey. My journal helps me to ask myself why I am working the way I currently am.

Make the Time

Finding the time and coordinating the schedules of busy people can be difficult. Yet it is essential to learn about new community change approaches and ideas. Here are three ideas that have helped many on their journey:

- If you have a staff position that provides time to work on community development, start by committing 10 percent of your time (a half-day a week) to learn, meet with people, and volunteer. Once you form a collaboration and you move into the common agenda phase of the work, consider moving this time allocation to 20 percent, or one day a week.

- Start by reading books and listening to podcasts with others in the community. Find conferences or seminars to attend, and invite others from your community or your organization to join you. The most important measure of your collective learning is the number of questions that arise for each of you. Ask "why?" together as often as you can.

• Increasingly people are joining collaboratives as volunteers. They may have an employer who will not give them time off to work on community change ideas. It is important to ensure that the learning journey is compatible with the schedule of volunteers.

Engage Your Upper-Level Leadership

Involve your board of directors, your boss, your funders, and your senior management team early in the journey toward whole community change. Find ways to help them learn with you and become engaged. This is not something you should leave until you have a plan. My experience is that the earlier you engage the people you report to, the greater the chance of them looking forward to the plan you will present later. Try providing them with ongoing updates and sending them articles or links to great podcasts so they will be engaged along the way.

My Wish for You

Most importantly, have fun learning together! In my coaching practice, I often say, "We should consider this journey more like hiking through a forest, as opposed to running on a treadmill." Be creative. Consider organizing experiential bus tours for your community to learn about the issue more deeply and to hear from the people most affected. Engage as often as possible with the people who are going to benefit the most if you are successful, especially those with living/lived experiences, and with people who are from completely different sectors.

Plan for good food and long breaks. Take walks together. Remember, at this stage of your community change process, you are learning together and building trusting relationships as you unthink and release old mental models and embrace new ways of thinking and working together.

3
Getting Started

*Never doubt that a small group of thoughtful com-
mitted citizens can change the world; indeed, it is the
only thing that ever has.*

—MARGARET MEAD

A GUIDE TO:

- Assessing your community's readiness for change
- Building your Leadership Team
- Creating an infrastructure and governance model

MARGARET MEAD'S POPULAR quote always
inspires me. Even though I still believe in the sentiment of the quote, I am convinced it is what this small
group of individuals "does next" that is going to change
the world. I say this not to be presumptuous, but rather to
emphasize that real change requires a lot of people to work
together, as a whole community, if lasting change is going
to occur.

A Getting Started Story

Liz Weaver, current Tamarack co-CEO, led a small group of leaders in Hamilton, Ontario. She was joined by Caroline Milne, CEO of the Hamilton Community Foundation, and Joanne Priel, General Manager of Community Services for the City of Hamilton. Hamilton had one of the highest rates of child poverty and health disparity in Canada. The early question for this small group of leaders was how to address the health disparities for low-income people. The question quickly changed to: How will we reduce poverty in our community?

These three individuals shared their vision for a better community with their friends, colleagues, service providers, and business leaders. The group began to grow. Next, they decided to hold focus groups and larger-scale community conversations that included people with lived/living experiences of poverty and compromised health. Though people were impressed by the reputation of the leaders, they were somewhat cynical about whether significantly reducing poverty was possible. The group was perplexed and wondered why people weren't more excited about what they were doing.

During one community conversation, a young lady stood up and said, "I find all this talk of reducing poverty helpful, but I have heard this all before. I am here because I want to help Hamilton to be the best place to raise my child." The room seemed to light up. There was new energy among the participants. People were animated and became passionate about this simple idea. "Hamilton: The best place to raise a child" became the name of their campaign and was eventually adopted as the city's vision; if you drove into Hamilton, every sign that welcomed you had this slogan. This once-small group added working groups, planning groups, and engagement groups. Together they worked to improve housing, healthcare, income, and employment opportunities. They also worked to improve the safety of low-income neighborhoods and health and educational outcomes. As their vision was adopted by the whole community, things began to change and Hamilton now has one of the lowest levels of child poverty in Canada.

A small group of people can change the world, but only by reaching out, engaging people in their vision, mobilizing people to act together, and growing the will of the community to want the change.

Is Your Community Ready for Change?

Large-scale community change requires certain conditions to thrive. At the Tamarack Institute, we adapted and simplified the ideas initially proposed by Paul Mattessich in his book *Collaboration: What Makes It Work*. We identified five key local conditions for success that we pose as lines of inquiry for a group embarking on a whole community change campaign:

- What is your community's history of collaboration?
- Are the positional leaders like politicians, service clubs, and CEOs engaged?
- Are funders engaged and interested in the change you seek?
- How important is the issue you are trying to solve for your community?
- If collaboration fatigue is high in your community, how will you address this?

This inquiry is important because it acts like a soil test for your garden. If you can answer all the questions affirmatively, then the "soil" for growing your whole community change campaign is healthy. Our experience is that many communities cannot answer all the questions affirmatively. There may be a high level of collaboration between local agencies working on the issue, but civic leaders and funders are not engaged with them as a group. A community might be far more interested in growing the economy than in improving the environment or health outcomes. Not receiving a perfect score on each question should not discourage you. Honestly answering each question will help you better understand how to improve the conditions to ensure your campaign will have the best possible chances for success. It's good to begin by gathering a group that includes funders, leaders in government, business, and social service as well as people with lived experiences. Through honest and authentic dialogue, the group can begin to home in on the most significant issues for change.

What Is Your Community's History of Collaboration?

When I assess a community's readiness for a whole community change campaign, I consider both the general and the specific collaboration history in the community. A campaign approach is important because it gives your initiative a focus and a sense of urgency. Understanding where collaboration is occurring, both past and present, is important. By taking stock of our community's collaborative history, we give credibility to the idea of working together to realize a whole community change. Existing collaboration in communities is often siloed or ad hoc. We are trying to break down segmented collaboration, engage more of the community, and develop ownership of a common agenda. Specific collaboration history helps to identify the key leaders in your community with effective skills who should be engaged in your campaign. It works to draw them together toward a common agenda and approach.

Considering the history of collaboration is helpful even if you find that there is minimal history of collaboration on the issue you hope to solve. One community discovered that most people they spoke with did not think their community was good at collaboration. In response, they started a collaboration awareness campaign and identified various community buildings—including the library, local arenas, and community gardens—that were built through collaborative action. Signs recognizing the collaborative efforts were posted at each site, and an annual collaboration award ceremony highlighted the best collaboration activities of the year.

HELPFUL TIPS

☐ Consider how collaborative your community is by listing some of the issues or projects that have been addressed collaboratively.

☐ Brainstorm the names of people who were involved in collaborative projects and take the time to interview some of those who led the process.

☐ Focus on the issue you are working on and consider how the people who care about the issue work together.

☐ Get to know the history of collaboration as well as the current state of collaboration around the issue you are addressing.

☐ Bring forward examples and identify the champions, community leaders, and funders who were involved.

☐ Identify potential challenges for collaboration.

☐ Consider how you plan to include everyone, including those with lived/living experience of the issue you are addressing.

Effective collaboration is essential for whole community change. A strong history of collaboration makes the work easier. But don't worry if your community does not have a collaborative history—that is all about to change.

Are the Positional Leaders Like Politicians, Service Clubs, and CEOs Engaged?

There are both formal and informal leaders in a community. The formal ones are those who have a specific title or status, such as the mayor of the city. Taking stock of formal leaders who are engaged reveals the status of the issue we want to address within the formal infrastructure of the community. To determine who is engaged, scan key local government leaders. We are looking for individuals who are already active in groups that support the issue. For example, we look for city council members who serve on the boards or are active in campaigns at the local food banks, job centers, or afford-able housing centers. We look for business leaders who have spoken out on poverty, have increased minimum wages for employees, or sit on boards that help those who are poor. As we identify these names, we want to record them as they will be excellent candidates for the Leadership Roundtable (LRT) we will form when building a common agenda. If they are currently not engaged, it is also important to understand the reasons they are not. Their reasons may eventually come up as obstacles for whole community involvement.

The informal leaders are those working in communities, coaching sports teams, directing choirs, teaching Sunday school, hosting birthday parties, and organizing neighbor-hood parties and fun days. We can identify the informal leaders more broadly in the common agenda phase. If we are struggling to identify the community leaders that care about the problem we are wanting to solve, we need to develop a community engagement strategy. I often suggest brainstorming the names of individuals and then inviting them to events or meeting them one-on-one. Most often I am surprised how many people do care about the issue we are hoping to solve and are willing to help. In other words, we are looking for the best assets (people) in the community who are concerned about the issues, are willing to learn and engage with others, and can commit to the breakthrough community change process.

HELPFUL TIPS

☐ Review some of the techniques identified in asset-based community development (ABCD) in Part II of this book. ABCD helps to ensure that the work is done by those who care versus by the professionals that want change.

☐ Identify leaders from four sectors including government, business, nonprofit, and people with lived/living experiences.

☐ Be sure to include people who have leadership roles that bring the credibility you need to be taken seriously in the community.

☐ Target individuals who have expressed interest in a collective impact approach to this issue.

☐ Seriously consider engaging individuals who will inspire others and evoke people's respect.

Are Funders Engaged and Interested in the Change You Seek?

Funders can be one of the greatest assets to a whole community change campaign, or they can be its greatest constraint. Funders have undue credibility in communities.

Without funding, it is very difficult to achieve whole systems change. Funders are slowly recognizing that they need to fund social innovation and are encouraging linked-up activities to address complex issues. Yet most often funders invest in issues that are easy to define and where the outcomes are very specific. I cannot overemphasize the importance of engaging funders early on in your campaign. Funders that are not on board can also be blockers of large-scale change in communities. As much as possible, involve the funders in every stage of your work. If possible, include some funders in your founding group of leaders. I suggest that you approach funders well before your campaign is made public. We want to seek their input and, if possible, include them on the Leadership Team. This is not the time to seek money but rather to deepen engagement by asking for advice and access to leadership contacts and data that they might have. Over time, as they become engaged, the funding will follow.

HELPFUL TIPS

- [ ] Identify appropriate organizations or individuals that fund services or solutions for the issue you are working on. Consider the United Way, foundations, corporations, and generous individuals.

- [ ] Consider how they are funding the work and approximately how much money is being invested in improving conditions.

- [ ] Bring the funders on board early and keep them engaged throughout the process.

- [ ] Talk with funders about their process of supporting community change and try to learn what they have discovered about the issue through past grants and initiatives.

How Important Is the Issue You Are Trying to Solve for Your Community?

Answering the preceding three questions will essentially answer this fourth one. At times the issue catches the attention of the community before it catches the attention of leaders. When seeking to understand if the issue matters, consider how often it is mentioned in the media. Consider how many people are attending community fundraisers supporting the issue. Consider if there are protests or other forms of community activism related to the issue occurring. If the issue is not a high priority for the community, consider how you are going to increase awareness. This is a good time to start thinking about your communications strategy.

HELPFUL TIPS

☐ Use community engagement techniques (described in Part II of this book) to identify individuals who care about the issue you want to see changed.

☐ Listen to how people are talking about the issue and how it is covered in the local media.

☐ Learn how other organizations give priority to the issue and how they are addressing it.

☐ Research how long the issue has been a priority for the community.

☐ Use local data reports to deepen understanding.

If Collaboration Fatigue Is High in Your Community, How Will You Address This?

There are often multiple collaborative teams active in a community. This is a positive sign that your community has a deepened understanding of the benefits of working together. It might result in your community being able to move much more quickly to implement your campaign. We have also seen the opposite effect, where community leaders are tired of collaborating. Community leaders feel they spend most of their time in meetings and do not have time for the essential work of their own organizations.

Collaboration fatigue is real. I am less convinced that it is a whole community issue but rather more an issue for some of the people who are very involved. I say that with some caution. It might be that multiple issues are being addressed at the same time. Or more likely, people have been involved in a collaboration that was very heavy on process and light on impact. In this case, it requires you to move more slowly. Some people will even tell you that you should not start your initiative because the community is too tired, or that you will be taking away from other campaigns. Rather than back down, it is best to slow down, reach out broadly, and ramp up your engagement strategy.

HELPFUL TIPS

☐ Take time to reach out to less involved community members or those that have been less active in community collaboration. I often find that business leaders and people with lived/living experience can be strong candidates.

☐ Seek to partner with an existing collaborative by forming an action team that would specifically address your issue.

☐ Before you announce your collaborative intention, take time to work quietly behind the scenes to build your community plan. Not all community engagement requires you to name your collaborative intention.

☐ Not all issues should be addressed as a community collaboration. Consider a different approach by narrowing your goals.

☐ Most importantly, be patient and wait for the community to find room for your ideas.

The common agenda process is easier and more effective when these conditions are considered and addressed. It's easier in that you have checked in with people who can either be supportive or difficult in moving the issue forward. It's more effective because you have taken the time to build community awareness of the high-profile and intensive campaign that is beginning to change your community. By addressing these five questions, you've set the stage to ensure that you will always have a unique mix of people involved. You have helped to ensure that the right people are involved. There is an unwritten assurance for all involved that this is a good thing and the right thing to do because the leaders are respected and credible within the community. Your community change work takes on a much higher priority and garners needed time and resources.

Remember, few communities have a perfect score when responding to these five questions. They are like a soil test. If you are weak in one area, then you need to spend more time there, possibly to shore up the number of community leaders or increase funders' engagement. Most importantly, by answering the previous questions you will get a sense of the people needed to form your Leadership Team.

Formalize Your Leadership Team

As you reach out to people and engage them in dialogue individually and in groups, you will sense a growing momentum.

When you have completed the assessment for readiness, you will have identified key leaders interested in collaborating for a whole community change. Leadership throughout the breakthrough community change process transforms itself over time. We begin, at this point in the process, by forming a Leadership Team.

The role of the Leadership Team at this stage includes:

- **Bringing multisector representation and credibility to the work.**   If possible, bring together a team made up of individuals from four sectors: government, business, non-profit, and people with lived/living experiences. I often recommend starting with two people from each sector. I also recommend that you agree on co-chairs, hopefully from two different sectors. In a whole community change process, the more diverse your Leadership Team is, the easier it is to engage people from diverse sectors as you work toward building a common agenda and implementing the community plan.

- **Identifying who you are and articulating the work you will do together.**   Early on, your team must develop a communication document, which is normally a short paper that describes who you are, the work you want to do, how you intend to work collaboratively, and the impact you want to achieve. It helps to have a document you can send to people when asking them to join a community conversation. We want to build community confidence in our approach as we explain our work. The Leadership Team is responsible for developing this document.

- **Developing and implementing a community engagement strategy.**   Our desire in a whole community change approach is to build a community that will work together and collectively improve outcomes. We do this by engaging everyone who cares by informing them, consulting with them, and involving them in the process. Developing an engagement plan helps us to be deliberate and focused. Using best practice community engagement strategies will help you to intentionally involve people from the community and build interest in your approach. Several community engagement strategies are described in Part II of this book.

- **Engaging in sensemaking together as you learn more about the issue.** Learning more about the issue requires hosting many community conversations and examining a lot of data. As the Leadership Team learns together, they will be able to deepen their understanding. I recommend that the Leadership Team work together to develop three documents:

  ○ A *data report* provides key statistics about the problem being addressed. This is often accompanied by key personal profiles of the different types of people affected by the issue.

  ○ An *asset report* includes the people and organizations that make your community strong in addition to a history of social innovation and caring.

  ○ A *case study review* identifies three or four communities that have addressed the issue you are working on using a whole community change approach. These case studies provide real evidence that change is possible.

- **Hosting community conversations.** Community conversations are an essential part of collaborative work. They can be a structured approach to bring many people into a common dialogue at the same time. The best conversations unite people in a common understanding of an issue while energizing them to act together. Bring different sectors together to talk and ask many questions. Start to host focus groups with people with lived/living experiences of the issues. Get as close to the issue as possible. Learn together as much as you can about whole community change and the complementary approaches, including collaborative leadership, collective impact, community engagement, community/social innovation, evaluating community change, and asset-based community development. Skills related to these approaches are described in Part II. To learn more about hosting community conversations, consider my book *Community Conversations: Mobilizing the Ideas, Skills, and Passion of Community Organizations, Governments, Businesses, and People.*

- **Engaging funders and considering financial needs going forward.**   The Leadership Team will want to reach out, engage, and involve funders early in the process. If you are new to the world of funders, a good place to begin is to talk to other nonprofit or community-based organizations that are working on the same issue as you are. Check out what foundations, government grants, or wealthy community members fund their work.

Organizing for Impact

One of the most important tasks for the Leadership Team is to determine a governance model that will sustain the work over time. A Leadership Team has at least three choices for governance. It is important for each community to seriously evaluate their situation and make the best decision based on their resources and needs.

First, they can organize without a formal structure. The strength of this model is that the team remains flexible and focuses on the work at hand rather than on organization building. This model is guided by the values and principles and does not include bylaws and articles of incorporation. It is a less threatening approach for community partners as the group focuses on engagement and learning activities. The limitations or constraints of this model are that informal structures often lack focus, especially if the structure remains informal into the action phase.

The second is to appoint an organization as the financial/legal sponsor. This sponsor will be able to receive funding, provide financial oversight, handle administration of human resources, and support any legal needs. The strength of this model is that funders feel they can trust the financial oversight of a well-respected organization. The limitations or constraints of this model are that the sponsor can be overly controlling of the collaboration and treat it as one of their projects as opposed to a community-led approach.

The third option is to incorporate and form a legal entity. The strength of this model is that as a legal entity it is easier to fundraise, plus it gives the work a sense of permeance. The limitations or constraints of this model are that incorporation can be perceived by community partners as a competing organization rather than a collaborating structure. It is also a time-intensive process that can develop slowly and take energy away from advancing the work.

I most often recommend that in the early stages of development the Leadership Team organizes as an informal structure. Once they are ready to hire staff or raise money, they connect with an organization to serve as their fiscal sponsor.

Margaret Mead was right. A small group of people can change the world if they are strategic and organized effectively. A small group of people builds community will and momentum. This is a highly creative time in the formation of the whole community change initiative. As you will read in the next chapter, this is a time to be curious, talk to everyone you can about the work you plan to do, and learn quickly as a Leadership Team.

As the Leadership Team forms, I am often asked, "When are we ready to develop a common agenda?" My answer is, "You have already started." You have convened a diverse group of leaders. You have defined your work. You have agreed on how you will work together. Most importantly, you have started to reach out to your community. You have created the container from which a common agenda can emerge and set the stage for breakthrough community change.

4

Creating a Common Agenda That Changes Everything

> *[The Tamarack Institute] emphasizes that the crucial thing these community-wide collective impact structures do is change attitudes. In the beginning, it's as if everybody is swimming in polluted water. People are sluggish, fearful, isolated, and looking out only for themselves. But when people start working together across sectors around a common agenda, it's like cleaning the water.*
>
> —DAVID BROOKS, *NEW YORK TIMES*, 2019

A GUIDE TO:

- Learning why a common agenda is not a strategic plan
- Shifting toward collective strategic thinking
- Implementing the five steps to a common agenda
- Creating a common agenda that changes everything
- Writing a community plan

B UILDING A COMMON COMMUNITY agenda is fundamental to breakthrough community change. It is the pathway to achieving a desired collective impact.

A common agenda has three primary purposes:

- First, the common agenda is a document that articulates the common understanding between network partners and describes what they have agreed to do together to change the community. The common agenda document includes the key goals and strategies for implementation. It is a statement of shared aspirations that unite us.

- Second, the common agenda provides a rationale for the goals the network partners have chosen to work on together. It is a way of sharing what the partners have learned about the broader community through research and consultations with diverse community members.

- Third, the common agenda is a road map for how network partners will work together. It includes a budget and a governance model.

Building a common agenda involves exploration and curiosity. It is about engagement, listening, and dialogue. The common agenda is about bringing together people who care about the identified issues and seek the desired change. If we think the way we have always thought, we will get what we always got. To build a common agenda, we need time to identify and release old patterns, explore, and accept new approaches and ideas. With a common agenda, we are a united force for change!

The Maine Cancer Foundation had the vision to reduce the effects of cancer by 20 percent in the state of Maine. They formed a network of organizational leaders to promote collaboration because they realized early on that connecting with their community and learning from people with lived experiences of cancer were essential. For nearly eighteen months they listened to their community, and twice during that time they brought together more than one hundred people to form a vision, engage in research, and join together to implement their vision. Then, with a common agenda agreed to by the whole community, they developed and launched their community plan.

The United Way of Central Iowa wanted to create a more equitable society. Though they implemented many programs to help those in need in their community, they wanted to develop a collective impact process to unite their community efforts. In addition to an extensive listening campaign, they brought their top one hundred leaders together to implement a vision they called Opportunities Central Iowa. Today nearly two hundred organizations meet quarterly to review their goals and monitor the progress of the network. Their common agenda is what unifies their whole community to work collectively toward their desired impact.

As recounted in Chapter 3, the municipality of Hamilton, Ontario, Canada, and the Hamilton Community Foundation joined together to tackle their most pressing issue: child poverty. Hamilton had the highest child poverty rate in Canada. By listening to their community and forming a network, a small group of key leaders launched a campaign called "Hamilton: The best place to raise a child." For more than two decades, this network has worked tirelessly to reduce child poverty and has achieved some impressive results. Their common agenda has sustained the efforts of the whole community.

A common agenda is a result of building trust in new ways and forging a shared commitment to the needed change. When people are committed to change, they bring forth organizational assets and contribute these to collective action. The process of developing a common agenda results in people being engaged, curious, and innovative. New creativity can be unleashed as people release old mental models and embrace collective ones. The process of building a common agenda results in a community uniting, bonding across sectors, and acting together for a better future.

A Common Agenda Is Not a Strategic Plan

In supporting dozens of groups to realize the breakthrough community change they sought, I have observed that the building of a common agenda is often misunderstood. Most organizational leaders have been trained to develop strategic plans. When they embark on a common agenda journey, they often "snap back" to strategic planning approaches. Strategic planning results in a highly regulated and efficient process of doing some version of an environmental scan, articulating a vision and key strategies, and developing an implementation plan with timelines. Often a small group will be formed to take on this task. Once the plan is complete, this small group presents this plan to their network and proceeds by "selling" the plan in hopes of achieving buy-in.

Strategic planning methods can be useful in building a common agenda's basic purpose. They are not effective in achieving the overarching purpose, which is community engagement and collective ownership of the plan. What we require is not more planning, but rather a process that results in collective strategic thinking and commitment. Henry Mintzberg, an important business academic and strategist, writes in his seminal *Harvard Business Review* article "The Fall and Rise of Strategic Planning" that the purpose of strategic planning is not just about putting together a plan—it's a creative process that helps everyone get onto the same page and document the common commitment.[1]

Strategic planning methods are often about developing a plan that is predictable, doable, and measurable. They are generally linear, provide a sense of organized control, and can be useful in outlining a basic purpose or plan. They are not effective in achieving community engagement and collective ownership of the common agenda. When we engage in strategic planning, we tend to think that a good plan is needed to work together. Mintzberg writes, "The problem is that [strategic] planning represents a calculating style of management, not a committing style." He believes that the purpose of strategic planning is not just about putting together a plan. He asks us to consider "a committing style" to engage people in a journey and to lead in such a way that everyone on the journey helps shape its course. As a result, enthusiasm inevitably builds along the way. He calls this strategic thinking. His ideas are at the heart of collective strategic thinking. What we require is not more planning, but rather a process that results in collective strategic thinking and an agreement that the purpose of strategic planning is more than just putting together a plan. We want a creative process that builds consensus and articulates the common commitment.

Collective Strategic Thinking

I cannot overemphasize how predominant the strategic planning model is and how overused it is in community change work. Nearly every group I have worked with in developing a common agenda has a challenge breaking out of the planning model mindset. As a result, they limit the role of creativity and intuition. They develop a strategic plan and limit collective strategic thinking.

To develop a common agenda, we first need to engage with one another. We need to discover, debate, and deliberate about the issue we are trying to improve. David Bohm, a theoretical physicist with a passion for understanding dialogue, states, "The goal is really to create a conversation that helps people to think together."[2] We need to create the space for thinking together in such a way that we can collectively discover the change that needs to occur.

I am fond of asking groups who are working on a common agenda the following questions: How many of you think that if we all just work a lot harder things are going to get better in our community? How about if we wrote just one more paper? Would it change things if we just got a little bit smarter? What if we spent a whole lot more money on the issue? Would this change things in the long term? The answer to all these questions is most often an emphatic no. So I ask: If working harder, smarter, and spending more money are not going to make things better in the long term, then what will?

In 2017 Des Moines was one of the wealthiest and fastest-growing cities in America and yet, as in most American cities, poverty was constant. Opportunities Central Iowa asked, How can we share opportunities in our community? They spent nearly eighteen months engaging their community and "holding" them to this question, which resulted in an amazing community plan. They allowed time for exploration and questioning to improve their thinking and break out of entrenched models of service delivery. They needed to take the time to build a common understanding and commitment to change. They needed to unite the community toward and build a common commitment to change. They created a common agenda and a community plan and then launched their campaign.

Building a Common Agenda

The very idea of agreeing on a common agenda requires involving a variety of people in debate and iterative discussions so that creativity and commitment have time to emerge, and new ideas can be embraced. These types of discussions build excitement. A good common agenda process acknowledges and builds on community assets. It considers the community's readiness to take on a collective impact idea, strengthens relationships, and deepens commitment.

Building a common agenda is about building a common commitment between stakeholders and a network of partners committed to bringing about change. Building a common commitment is primarily about deepening relationships, learning together, and sharing common experiences. We want to move from a place of "I know what to do, listen to me" to a place of questioning "Why, with everything we know, are things not getting better?" Over time we want to move toward a collective knowing. If we work together in this new way, we will get better outcomes.

Building a common agenda is about reaching out to our community, finding those who care about the issue, and bringing everyone into the conversation. It is not just about experts, professionals, and all those who are paid to care about the problem; we must also involve those with lived/living experiences of the issues. If we are working to reduce poverty, we must engage with people experiencing poverty and listen to their stories and ideas. When we want to improve graduation rates, we need to talk to more than teachers and school administrators; we need to talk to the students themselves— especially those who are struggling and have not graduated— and their parents. When we involve everyone who cares, we broaden our scope of engagement. We create a "hive mind" where everyone shares collective wisdom and benefits from collective intelligence.

A common agenda is about evoking our curiosity and creativity. I have already spoken about how a strategic planning mentality turns a common agenda journey into a process of efficiency and limits creativity. In their desire to be efficient, people implement a strict planning process that shuts down people's ability to imagine, explore, and discover. Ideas are controlled and input is often quantified and grouped. I keep reminding groups that it only takes one good idea to change everything. The difficulty is that finding that specific good idea requires a wide variety of voices and a willingness to let the new idea emerge.

A common agenda requires us to take the time for broad engagement to build widespread agreement. One of the most common challenges groups face is assigning dedicated people to lead the commitment process. Everyone is busy with their jobs. Often groups will hire a contract staff person from outside the network. The disadvantage of this option is that often this person does not have the key relationships to mobilize a network. Another option is to ask network partners to do this work on top of what they are already doing. The disadvantage of this option is that tasks are often rushed and, as one of my colleagues is fond of saying, work "falls off the edge of the desk." Broad engagement requires a plan, hours of work, and a firm commitment. As I have said, you have to find what works for your community.

Implementing:
Five Steps to a Common Agenda

I recommend a five-step approach to develop a common agenda for breakthrough community change. As mentioned earlier, my way is not necessarily the right way. It is just one way to success. I ask that you use it to form your own best way forward that works for your community.

I recommend this five-step approach because I so often see groups "spinning" for their first year. They are often not sure what to do, so they spend a lot of time talking within a very small, inward-looking group. This is exhausting. Many groups just give up and the leaders drop away. Another reason I recommend this five-step approach is to overcome the tendency many leaders have toward the efficient strategic planning approach that I described earlier. The approach I recommend ensures that you are identifying and engaging key people in your community very early in the process. Finally, this approach is both motivating and action-oriented. It gives leaders a strong sense that there is momentum and that they are making progress.

And yes, I get the irony of asking you not to use a prescriptive strategic planning process and then writing a seemingly prescriptive five-step program. Please modify this approach to one that works for you.

Step 1: Form the Leadership Team

Form a small Leadership Team that will work together for twelve to eighteen months and whose members are tasked with engaging the community and creating a widely owned common agenda for your work.

There is a lot of work to do in developing a common agenda for breakthrough community change. It is a full-time job for at least two people in most communities. Most networks do not have the money to hire these people early in the process, and even if they do, newly hired people do not normally have the kind of connections and community knowledge to bring key leaders together. The team I recommend is most often made up of people who are already dedicating a percentage of their time to the common agenda process. One person may get a 50 percent time allocation from their organization for one year; another may get 25 percent; and so on. Some networks hire one person to do most of the heavy lifting and bring on four or five people who have a percentage of their time allocated by their organizations to do the work at hand. The more we can formalize the time allocation commitment of each team member, the higher the probability of getting the work done well.

Step 2: Identify and Gather Your Top One Hundred Leaders

Identify and bring together key leaders from the four key sectors (government, business, nonprofit, and people with lived/ living experiences). This diverse group of leaders comprises the people who will most likely work together to implement your community plan and are critical to effective and expansive support of the campaign.

As early as you can, identify and bring together your top influencers who care about this issue. With most groups I use the Top 100 Exercise, which you can easily find on the Tamarack Institute website or in my book *Community Conversations*. This exercise will help you identify your top twenty-five leaders from each of the four main sectors: government, business, nonprofit, and people with lived/living experiences. It is important that your invitation is broad and goes beyond just those organizations with a formal mandate around the issue.

For example, if your goal is to reduce the effects of cancer in your community, you will want to include the following:

- Community organizations and people from hospitals and community health centers, as well as doctors, nurses, support and counseling organizations, advocates, and so on.

- Business leaders who have shown an interest in the issue of cancer. Look for companies that have sponsored events or funded cancer-related organizations or business leaders you know who have had cancer or have a personal relationship with someone who has cancer.

- Government leaders representing a local municipality or city, region, state, or province, or even nation. The broader the players, the better.

- People who are experiencing cancer or who are survivors; ensure that this group makes up at least 25 percent of your top one hundred.

When you gather your key leaders (top one hundred) from the four sectors (whole system) together early in your community change process, your work will feel like it is leaping forward. People will start talking and a new sense of hope will emerge. People will begin to get involved and help.

You can gather the last two groups at the same time. Listening to your community slows everything down (in a good way) and provides an opportunity for you to truly hear the stories of people affected by your issue. You will be collecting the wisdom of everyone who cares, and at the same time, you will broaden engagement.

Step 3: Implement a Common Engagement Strategy

Implement a broad-based community engagement strategy to hear your community and launch a "listening to your community" campaign. To achieve collective impact, we need a growing community of people willing to implement change. This happens primarily through asking people to share their ideas to help us understand the current state of the issue and what changes people feel are necessary to achieve better outcomes. Many groups I work with form a Listening Team, a group dedicated to reaching out to the community to listen and engage them. Initially, they work together to identify key partners who might cohost a consultation.

One of the goals is to involve people who have direct experience of the issue being explored. For example, if reducing cancer, involve people who have survived cancer and family members who have walked the journey with them. If reducing poverty, involve the working poor, homeless individuals and families, people using the food banks, and people at the local health clinic. The voices and ideas of people with lived experience enhance and often transform the discussion with leaders from public and private sector agencies.

The Top 100 Exercise described in step 2 makes the work of the Listening Team much easier. People who attend the gathering have a good understanding of the issue and have spent time talking with others about it. They recognize the need for broad-based consultation and are willing to help us organize consultations.

The "listening to your community" campaign often takes four to six months and has two functions. First, we need to hear what people think needs to change. Second, we need to broaden engagement. Many groups will hear from more than five hundred people, and some as many as one thousand. The database for the network grows substantially. The communications they share connect people and often generate excitement and hope. For many networks, the listening campaign is when they begin to feel that a collective impact is possible.

Step 4: Develop Action Teams and Early Win Strategies

Develop short-term Action Teams with mandates of no more than six months to implement early win strategies. Action

Teams are small groups of people dedicated to implementing your impact ideas.

At about the six-month point, most networks implementing a collective impact process experience tremendous pressure to implement ideas that lead to concrete action. People are weary from talking. We know that a lot of talking—and learning— is critical to developing new and innovative ideas. Yet, as one of my clients reminded me, "there are thinkers and there are doers, and we need them both."

One of the best ways to harness this pressure to prioritize doing over talking is to implement Action Teams that have a six- to twelve-month mandate to implement concrete actions. Quick-win ideas will arise in the gathering discussed in step 2. They will also arise as the Listening Team holds consultations.

Quick-win Action Teams provide concrete action at a time in our process when we are gathering information and writing about our accomplishments. I have observed many quick-win Action Teams, such as the following:

- To reduce cancer rates, a quick-win Action Team was formed to work with employers to host an early screening day where employers gave their employees with "risks" time off to go for tests.

- To improve access to affordable housing, a quick-win Action Team was formed to work with landlords to find better housing for "the easiest 10 percent to place" of people on the subsidized housing registry.

- To improve food security, a quick-win Action Team was formed to recruit people living in poverty to harvest and preserve fresh vegetables in season.

Step 5: Write Your Community Plan

Write your community plan. Present the plan and solicit partnerships with your top one hundred people and the organizations they represent.

Most community plans are written within twelve to eighteen months of a network forming. A community plan is the result of a community agreeing on what they want to do together. It is the written commitment of their common agenda. I encourage groups to take their time in writing a community plan for three reasons:

- In the first year, community leaders need to release from their current thinking and way of working. It takes time to learn to work together, understand a systems approach to change, and find new synergies between network partners.

- The first year is a time for emergence, where new ideas come easily and there is heightened creativity and hope. This can be a highly productive period for new ideas to form, new actions to take shape, and collective wisdom and intelligence to emerge.

- Writing a community plan is about agreeing on what we want to do together. Often this means that groups will agree on large strategic ideas. The action plan that follows is often not addressed until we move into the implementation phase. This is a time for agreeing collectively on the work ahead of us. This takes debate and compromise and requires trusting relationships to be formed. We also need our community network to sign on to the plan.

I encourage networks to write a five-year community plan. I know this sounds like a long time, and that many leaders often develop three-year strategies. I like five years because, from experience, it takes a year to fully implement the plan. By the end of year two, you move toward peak outputs. Years three and four are peak output years when you get the most impactful results. Year five is for wind-down, transition, or renewal. While a five-year plan helps to simplify the framing of the process, we should recognize that collective impact initiatives can take ten or more years to address issues depending on how deeply rooted the issues are. The time frame is a guide, not a prescription.

The community plan should capture our common agenda and include the following elements:

A listing and acknowledgment of all the partners. The most important reason for a collaborative impact is to bring a network of partners into focus around an issue so we can collectively achieve better outcomes. This plan is the collective agreement of what we will do together.

Who we are and what we want to accomplish. The Leadership Team will have already developed a document that included a written description. The network will have adopted this definition early in the process. We now need to update it for our plan, as most likely our statement of purpose and outcomes has grown and deepened.

The story of our last twelve months. I like the community plan to tell the story of the formation and give some details about the process taken to achieve a common agenda.

A data report: Moving toward shared measurement. Before the first gathering of the partners (see steps 1 and 2), we wrote several short papers, which were used throughout the first year and have formed much of the base information needed for a collaborative impact.

A summary of these papers should be in your community plan. I find it easier to focus on comprehensive shared measurement in the first year of implementation. The community plan should include key measures identified through consultations and research that are important to the network of partners.

A listening report.   For almost a year the Leadership Team has reached out to the community. A description of this process and what you learned should be in the community plan.

Key strategic directions and strategies.   One of the most important sections in the community plan is an articulation of the broad strategic directions you will work on together and the specific strategies you will implement over the next three to five years. It is helpful to describe the desired outcomes for each strategic direction outlined in the community plan.

A governance plan.   The infrastructure for breakthrough community change is typically made up of the fiscal sponsor (who can accept donations and has exemplary HR and financial policies), a staff team, a Leadership Roundtable, and Work Teams. The plan should articulate how the governance capacity will be created.

A budget.   Funds are required to effectively implement a collaborative impact. An operational budget (revenue sources, staff, and expenses) and a short fundraising plan are extremely helpful, as they give notice to donors that an ask is imminent.

Writing a community plan and presenting the common agenda to your network and the broader community is a tremendous achievement. When it is done well, you will probably have the following outcomes:

- The community takes ownership of the plan. There is a willingness to implement the plan together.
- Key leaders have endorsed your plan, and this provides credibility in the broader community.
- Funders are interested in funding the plan.
- You have presented a strong case for support. You have articulated the need for action, the need for a collaborative response, and the need for the key strategies.

The result of rushing a common agenda, or minimizing our efforts in consultation and broad engagement, is that we draft a plan that needs to be "sold" to our network. We have not built community will and our issue is seldom a community priority.

Creating a common agenda and writing this down in the form of a five-year community plan can change everything if you do it in a way that mobilizes a community toward action. To change everything, we need to create the conditions that will result in a collective impact. To change everything in a community requires a large group of people from different sectors working together. Broad community support is required to achieve system-changing outcomes. If you do the work of building a common agenda well, the work of implementation is much easier, and you have a greater probability of impact.

5

The Campaign Phase: Implementing Your Strategy

You need a strategy for getting results . . . you need to organize for success.

—LIZ WEAVER AND MARK CABAJ IN CONVERSATION

A GUIDE TO:

- Keeping the momentum going
- Setting goals and establishing target outcomes
- Translating the common agenda into a work plan
- Finding a legal/fiscal sponsor and expanding infrastructure
- Shifting to a campaign implementation Leadership Roundtable
- Establishing Work Teams
- Developing an engaged strategy and a communications strategy

---

I REMEMBER GETTING AN EMAIL FROM a community leader I was coaching. Her group was now moving toward the implementation phase of their strategy and she was worried. She wrote, "We have spent nearly a year developing a common agenda for our community; now what? People want action. They want to see immediate results. The reality is that change takes time and money. We have limited staff and certainly nowhere near the resources needed to realize the goals in our strategy. How do we organize ourselves to get results?"

This is a typical sentiment for groups I have worked with. Implementing your plan can be challenging. Moving from the common agenda phase to the implementation or campaign phase is a major shift.

Most often the common agenda phase of the work results in a remarkable year mobilizing the community and elevating the issue as a priority for your community. Your community partners will have shown tremendous leadership in the community and are united toward a collective action. You may even feel that your community is on the verge of a breakthrough.

Now that your community has agreed to some ambitious goals, you will want to find creative ways to move the energy of the group away from planning and organizing and toward implementation. You need to organize in such a way that there is something for everyone to do. Just as you took the time to support the community to rethink your community's approach, you need to move the whole community toward common action. You need to build on the common commitment you have already achieved if you want a breakthrough.

Building on the Momentum

You are now moving from the common agenda phase to the campaign phase of your work. The common agenda phase builds momentum around ideas for change in the hope that a better future is possible. The process you used to engage your community in a common agenda has resulted in significant engagement and hopefully a significant number of names in your database. Key leaders have emerged, as well as funders. You have elevated your idea to be an important priority in your community.

The most important work now is to keep that momentum building and involve as many people as possible in the implementation of the plan. I recommend you treat this stage as a campaign.

The Campaign Phase

The campaign phase is where you will operationalize the strategies developed in the common agenda phase. Now you will set goals and establish target outcomes. You must do this in a way that excites and energizes people. In the next five years, you will achieve something spectacular! A bold plan is critical to motivating people to action.

A campaign motivates people and is highly effective in sustaining momentum. My experience is that people like to be involved in campaigns. Establishing a specific time frame for the work, setting annual targets, and reporting on the results are all steps that help people roll up their sleeves and dig into the work. Strategies can be adjusted as the work evolves. As the campaign progresses, people will feel a sense of action that results from the long process of community conversations and the development of the common agenda.

Communities typically choose a three- or five-year campaign time frame. Often communities state a larger goal or bold vision that may take ten or more years to achieve, setting interim targets along the way. These interim targets can be milestone markers of outcomes for a certain number of years. For example, a campaign might set interim targets for annual outcomes or longer-range targets of three to five years within the total campaign of ten years. It is typical to develop a renewal or wind-down plan in the last year of the campaign. In Chapter 9 we talk more about campaign renewal and wind-down.

A campaign builds the momentum needed for a break-through. My experience is that in a five-year campaign many communities achieve most of their outcomes in the final two years. During the first few years, a community is learning rapidly and adjusting its plan. Community leaders engage more deeply over time. Needed policy changes are discovered, and there is a growing consensus that these changes are necessary to improve the quality of life for the community. Key actions supported by policy changes create an opportunity for significant change outcomes at the population level.

Finally, funders are supportive of multiyear campaigns. When a specific time frame is presented, donors and grantors can more easily envision how their contribution will make a difference, and outcome projections feel more real to funders.

Moving from the common agenda phase to the campaign phase requires transitions.

Transitions

There are six transitions required to move from the common agenda phase to the campaign phase. I want to discuss how you can use the accomplishments achieved in the common agenda phase to build the momentum needed for bold action.

1. Translating the Common Agenda into the Community Plan

Your community plan has been widely endorsed and has broad ownership. You want to translate the common agenda into a comprehensive work plan that gives everyone engaged something to do and keeps them moving forward. It is now time to transition the key strategies in the community plan into actions and define the specific outcomes. This requires you to develop formal and informal opportunities for action.

In your community plan, you have an analysis, a vision, and key strategies that the community leaders have agreed on together. You now need to organize Work Teams around each strategy and develop formal action plans that will realize these strategies:

- Each Work Team will take the time to develop their own "pictures of impact" that clearly articulate the actions they plan to undertake.

- Plan with the end in mind. The role of the Leadership Roundtable (LRT) is to consolidate each Work Team's pictures of impact (theory of change) into one organizational plan. This plan is your new road map.

- The role of the LRT at this stage is to be the keepers of the vision and help all the Work Teams stay active and stay focused.

- Whole community change cannot happen through the formation of Work Teams alone. You will need to develop a strategy to communicate with your broad range of supporters and provide them with a call to action.

- Often this call to action is embedded in your communications strategy. How are you going to keep building your networks of supporters? You will invite them to learn together and make changes. You are seeking input into policy discussions. You are inviting your supporters to community celebrations. You are also asking them to share their stories of change.

- Work Teams will develop action ideas that might directly support people to improve their lives, or they might work on policy changes that will improve conditions for those most affected. In the spirit of campaigns, you also want them to consider approaches that might help many people become involved. An example of ending poverty is a campaign for employers to declare themselves as living wage employers, or asking faith communities to move "just one" family out of poverty using a wraparound model of support. The more of these campaign-type strategies we employ, the greater opportunity you create for everyone in the community to change just a little bit.

2. Finding a Legal/Fiscal Sponsor

You now want to transition the community sponsor you had put in place during your common agenda phase. You will either find a new campaign phase sponsor or transition the role of your existing sponsor so they can act as the legal sponsor as you implement your plan.

- You will need to decide if the organization that sponsored the work through the common agenda phase is the right legal/fiscal sponsor as you move forward to implement the plan.
- You will need the legal/fiscal sponsor to be an organization that has good financial and human resource systems and can accept donations and grants.
- You will need to ask the sponsor to appoint two people to the LRT. Typically, I recommend they appoint their CEO and a member of their board.

- The sponsor agrees to manage the financial and human resource aspects of your campaign.

- The sponsor agrees that they will allow the LRT to focus on strategies and implement the plan.

3. Establishing a Campaign Implementation Roundtable

You will need to transition your common agenda LRT to a highly engaged campaign LRT. This is a good time to review your LRT membership.

- You formed a team during the startup and common agenda phase. Their skills and focus helped the community to work together to develop new and bold ideas, achieve a common agreement, and implement the community plan.

- This is a good time to ask those members if they want to continue to be on the LRT or if they would prefer to take on another role. I have found implementing a plan requires different skills than developing a plan. Typically, in my experience about half of your LRT will move to different roles, such as the Work Teams, giving you room to add some new members. You may also want to grow the Roundtable size and add more members.

- The new LRT in the implementation phase will take on the following tasks:

  ○ Develop and agree on a governance model for your work and negotiate the terms with your legal sponsor.

  ○ Ensure the members of the LRT are diverse and represent business, government, nonprofit, and people with lived/living experiences.

- ° Appoint two co-chairs who are willing to facilitate meetings. Form an executive team that will handle the day-to-day operations of the campaign and establish the agendas for Roundtable meetings.

- ° Hire any staff—most importantly, the executive director.

- ° Appoint chairs for all the committees.

The new LRT plays the strategic role of pacing the work of the campaign. They review the reports of the Work Teams and serve as a unifying force. They also advance the ongoing work of community engagement and support the work teams to advance their work.

4. Establishing Work Teams

You want to transition your Action Teams that were established in the common agenda phase and form Work Teams. The role of these teams is to implement the key strategies identified in the common agenda phase. Implementing these strategies will focus the work of the campaign phase. After the LRT appoints the chairs (or better yet co-chairs) of these Work Teams, they will support the newly appointed chairs in recruiting team members. These Work Teams are to implement the key strategic directions.

Each team is made up of people from diverse backgrounds and includes members with business, government, nonprofit, and lived/living experience. You want members with strong interest and influence around the issues in the community. Suppose the strategy they are working on is to increase the supply of affordable housing in the community. The members would include people from the construction trades; landlords; government leaders that manage or fund affordable housing;

community leaders that care for users of affordable housing; funders of affordable housing; and people that currently live in, have previously lived in, or need affordable housing.

- Each team will agree on the key actions necessary to implement the strategic priority they are leading. I strongly recommend that each Work Team develop pictures of impact or a theory of change that helps them to make a direct connection between the actions they are planning and the change they hope to see. They will want to create these pictures of impact to articulate how people are living better lives because of your activity and to articulate the systems change you want to see in the community.

- Each team will identify the community partners needed to implement the strategy and ensure those partners are engaged. Typically, you will rely on these community partners to carry out the work identified in the plan.

- Each team will build relationships with funders and submit proposals for funding key actions.

- Each team will engage both strategic influencers and people with lived/living experiences to ensure that there is ongoing communication and community will for the change needed.

5. Developing an Engaged Strategy

You want to transition your engagement strategy to ensure leaders stay engaged. Through the common agenda phase, you have built a large number of engaged leaders for the work and the proposed change. You need both an *engagement* strategy to continue to build community will for change and an *engaged* strategy to keep supporters active and engaged.

6. Developing a Communications Strategy

You want to transition your communications strategy to advance your campaign approach. In the common agenda phase, you built a large database of supporters and implemented an effective communications strategy to keep everyone informed. This work needs to continue throughout the campaign phase. You will need an internal communications strategy that focuses on keeping all agencies and individuals that provide direct support for the issues informed about the work. You will also need an external communications strategy that focuses on agencies and individuals who will be learning about your efforts and the issues and potentially joining the effort. The external communications strategy will help to grow your influence in the community.

The internal communications strategy involves the LRT and the Work Teams and focuses on carefully developing pictures of impact or theories of change, describing the effect and impact of the actions taken, and preparing this information for public sharing through the external communications strategy.

There are three goals of the internal communications strategy:

- The first goal involves the LRT and the picture of impact or theory of change they develop for the entire campaign. A picture of impact describes the work you want to do together. If the goal is to reduce poverty, the picture of impact describes how the community will look after three or five years of activity. It goes on to describe the change you want to see in some detail, how you think this change will occur, and the key activities that you believe will realize that change. Finally, it provides a plan for how those activities will be implemented. The picture of impact acts as a guide for all the Work Teams.

- The second goal involves the Work Teams. Each Work Team also develops a picture of impact. As mentioned earlier, if the strategy is to develop more affordable housing in the community, then the Work Team will specifically describe the impact of their work, who will be affected, and the desired change for the community. You will go on to provide details of the work necessary to achieve that change with a plan.

- The third goal is to bring Work Team reports to the LRT quarterly. The LRT reviews the activities and progress made toward their desired impact and then uses these reports to support the external communications strategy.

The external communications strategy is all about building momentum and influence by reporting to all agencies and individual supporters in an ongoing way. Supporters are those people in your database who have participated to date and have given you their email addresses as permission to communicate with them. A newsletter, a website, news stories, and direct mail letters are often used for this purpose. Like its internal counterpart, the external communications strategy also has three goals:

- The first goal is to share information that describes the activities you want to see more of with your active supporters. This is a very powerful opportunity to showcase what your team has identified in your picture of impact and agreed will result in the desired change.

- The second goal is to demonstrate the growing momentum for the work clearly and publicly. This includes demonstrating the volume of activity and reporting on key outcomes.

- The third goal is to share with your supporters what
  you are learning and how you are using this learning
  to achieve your outcomes and make an impact in the
  community. Continuous communication gives agencies
  and individuals in the community the sense that they
  are part of something new, exciting, alive, and evolving.
  It also allows more agencies and individuals to join and
  feel that they are part of the change they want to see.
  Hosting community conversations, keynote speakers,
  learning workshops, or seminars can greatly increase
  commitment and involvement.

6

Organizing for Impact

Leaders play unique roles in community change efforts. They navigate from the middle, engaging community champions to drive forward the change, and also coordinate the efforts of community-based partners to align their programs and services.

—LIZ WEAVER

A GUIDE TO:

- Understanding the role of leadership
- Developing a staff team
- Expanding funding
- Maintaining ongoing communication with the community

THERE ARE MANY TRANSITIONS AS you move from the common agenda phase of your work to the campaign phase. The common agenda phase, if executed effectively, provides you with the foundation you need for success. The campaign phase shifts your focus. You are now moving your thinking from planning to doing. You are embracing a campaign mindset.

At this stage of your change process, you have already accomplished so much:

- A community plan is now an action plan with key steps for implementing your ideas and moving your work toward impact.

- A community sponsor is now your legal/fiscal sponsor, which allows you to receive funds and gives you the credibility you need to scale your work and expand your staff team.

- A common agenda Leadership Roundtable (LRT) is now an implementation LRT, giving you an organizational structure that advances action and outcomes.

- Action Teams are now Work Teams that are enacting the strategies you have developed.

- An engagement strategy has grown to include an engaged strategy that provides key steps to keeping your leadership engaged.

- A communications strategy now includes an internal communications plan and an external communications plan. These plans give you the actions needed to ensure everyone stays connected and on the same page.

- You are well on your way toward moving from planning to impact.

There are just five more areas we want to consider as we move fully into the campaign phase of our work.

Leadership

Moving the work of engagement and planning to action and impact is often difficult for organizations. As shared in the previous chapter, working toward action and impact takes a different set of skills and requires different actions than community engagement and planning. One group I was coaching decided to give the co-chairs of their LRT specific roles. One chair led the ongoing engagement work and what she called "the people" side of the campaign, while the other co-chair took on the responsibility of what she called "the impact" side of the work.

The impact work was new to the organization but not completely new, as Action Teams in the common agenda phase had also developed short-term impact plans. After the LRT asked each Work Team to develop pictures of impact that would guide their actions, the impact-focused co-chair created or modified a unified picture of impact that would encompass all the strategies. The LRT then created a Work Team executive group, made up of the chairs of each of the Work Teams, that would meet monthly to report on activities, progress, and impact (our APIs) and to identify synergies that were developing between the strategies. This group also acted as a great team to brainstorm ideas and solutions for problems other teams may have been facing. This was a very effective approach. Meanwhile, the co-chair that was leading engagement focused most of her time on ensuring that people were active and engaged. She did this by forming a specific Engagement and Communications Team. This co-chair was also skilled in raising money and developed a fundraising team that also met monthly.

There are always administrative details, such as approving budgets and hiring staff. An Executive Team was made up of the two co-chairs, a representative from the legal/fiscal sponsor, and the lead staff person for the project. This ensured that the LRT was not burdened with making operational decisions.

The Staff Team

During the common agenda phase, most groups will hire temporary staff or consultants to help them with research, writing, and coordination. Sometimes staff from the organization partners will assume these responsibilities at no cost. During the campaign phase, you will need more staff capacity.

Ideally, you will want three full-time roles: a Team Lead, a Project Officer, and a Communications/Administrative Officer. In smaller communities, these roles are typically part-time or volunteer-supported, whereas larger communities will often hire multiple project officers.

TEAM LEAD

The Team Lead works very closely with the co-chairs of the LRT and supports their work. This person:

- Engages with senior community leaders
- Works with fundraising efforts
- Provides staff direction
- Leads planning exercises
- Implements the communications and engagement plans
- Supports the chairs of the Work Teams
- Conducts community presentations

PROJECT OFFICER

The Project Officer works with and takes direction from the Team Lead. This person:

- Supports the Work Team meetings (including scheduling and note-taking)

- Provides research and technical support
- Ensures the actions of the Work Teams are implemented
- Works with volunteers to advance policy and systems change
- Provides ongoing staff support to the Work Teams

COMMUNICATIONS/ADMINISTRATIVE OFFICER

The Communications/Administrative Officer takes direction from the Team Lead. This person:

- Manages the database
- Supports volunteer engagement
- Produces communication materials (such as a newsletter)
- Supports the communications and engagement plan
- Manages social media
- Works with volunteers and staff to produce stories and thought pieces
- Supports large event planning and implementation

Recruiting Staff

Staff roles are an essential part of community change. If these roles are filled by volunteers, you will need to be very clear about the knowledge, experience, and time commitment required for these positions. In my experience, staff can be recruited in three ways:

- Partner organizations or even the sponsoring organization can fulfill one or all of the roles described. This is often the case in smaller communities where fund-raising is more challenging. A hybrid model also exists where one staff person is hired and essentially does some work in all the roles, but does not do all the work. Partner organizations may take on the database, producing communications materials and booking meetings in a space they provide.

- You can hire the three positions, who then become employees of the legal sponsor but who report to the co-chairs and the executive of the LRT. This may require a budget of upward of $250,000 (in 2022 dollars).

- You can also contract out various roles fulfilled by staff, and this would work similarly to the first approach.

With staff support, volunteers can work less at keeping things organized and can focus on the impact level of the work, especially those tasks that utilize their vast community connections.

Raising Money

There are two primary reasons to raise money:

To fund operations. You are going to need some operating money to implement a large-scale change initiative. Whole community change requires staff. These staff can be provided by the collaborative partners, but most groups hire at least one staff person. You are also going to need money for hosting meetings, buying coffee and sandwiches, and possibly hiring outside expertise.

To fund projects. If you are looking to end poverty, one of the systemic changes you want to enable is that more money is available in your community for the breakthrough community change initiatives you have envisioned. These funds can come in the form of small grants or larger, multiyear grants.

Raising money for both operations and projects requires you to build relationships with funders. If there is only one thing you take away from this conversation, it is that raising money should never be an afterthought. You will need to engage funders at the very beginning of your initiative. One of the four preconditions for success we discussed earlier is that you want to ensure that funders care about the issue you are working on. This implies that you have been talking to funders all along and that funders have been part of the early action teams and have sat on your LRT. If you are not able to have funders commit to being part of your LRT, then assign an LRT member to meet with key funders at least quarterly.

Funders will typically be ready to invest in your project ideas as you enter the campaign phase if you have engaged them from the beginning. Funders are often wealthy families, successful companies, foundations, and various levels of government. As you consider learning more about fundraising for your campaign, consider taking some online classes or find a mentor that will help you learn the techniques in major donor fundraising. My experience is that major donors, especially successful entrepreneurs, are most motivated to give.

Shifting money is an equally important part of your campaign. One aspect of system change is to direct more funding toward the desired solution you are proposing. If you want to end poverty, you will want to shift the system priorities from primarily providing those who are poor with temporary financial relief to directing some of those monetary resources toward ending poverty. This can be done in two ways. First, you can help partner agencies change their mandate from specifically relieving poverty to adding in the work of ending poverty. An example of this is a food bank that shifted from simply handing out food to developing a "food co-op" model in which they actively recruit recipients of food to volunteer at the food bank so that they can learn key job skills (driving a forklift, operating a cash register, packing shelves, sorting, filling orders). Second, you can advocate for funders to move money away from agencies that work only to support direct service to those that both provide services and connect directly to the work of systems for large-scale change. Of course, this is tricky and requires a lot of dialogue with both agencies and their funders.

Communication and Celebration

There is one more thing I want to share that I hope will help the campaign phase flourish. The campaign phase succeeds when we are deliberately building community momentum for change. Most importantly, you want to keep the community informed of the progress of your campaign. You do this by regularly sending out communications, such as a newsletter. Do not neglect your database. I suggest that you have a target built into your communications plan for the growth of your database. The more people you can directly communicate with, the better. Your social media accounts should have similar targets.

Bringing your partners together quarterly is also essential. Hosting a quarterly gathering around a variety of topics is an excellent way to keep people committed. The meeting might start with some words of gratitude, a success story, and a campaign update. Then a speaker or trainer would share ideas followed by discussion at multisector roundtables.

Deliberately celebrating the work of the collective is critical not only for people to feel appreciated but also to keep the spirit of the initiative positive. Learning together through ongoing dialogue shows the community that the issue you are working on together is complicated and that learning and change are critical prerequisites to innovating as a community. Monitoring key data points and reporting on these regularly is also essential to building momentum.

Building momentum, organizing, and communicating well accelerate impact.

7
Getting to Impact Mindsets

Management is doing things right; leadership is doing the right things.

—PETER DRUCKER

A GUIDE TO:

- How emergence thinking helps you adapt
- How comprehensive community change helps you see the whole picture
- Why collective innovation thinking is essential
- How policy changes are required for breakthroughs
- Mobilizing lots of change
- A "getting to maybe" approach

IF GETTING TO IMPACT WERE as simple as having a great idea, developing a plan, and managing that plan to success, I am pretty sure all the needs in our community would be met. Social change is messy and complex, and it requires leadership. Community challenges are often adaptive. We focus on better wages and improving food security, only to have a major employer close their business or the government change an important program that supports those in need. Just as we get to what we think is a better way, something changes. Leadership is constantly adapting, learning, and changing.

This chapter is different than the previous ones in that it is less how-to and more a set of ideas and principles—what I call *mindsets*—that I have found extremely helpful in moving a breakthrough community change toward impact. In simplest terms, I have never seen a campaign go as planned. You are required to adjust and adapt constantly. I want to introduce you to six mindsets that I have found useful for getting to impact.

Plan–Do–Adjust

Earlier in this book, I wrote about the initiative I founded to reduce poverty in Waterloo, Canada. We raised a lot of money. We mobilized important leaders in the government, business, and nonprofit sectors. We engaged many people with lived and living experiences. We had very active and engaged Work Teams and an amazing staff team. Our partners had implemented dozens of new projects. We could feel the momentum building in our community. Yet after nearly two years, we could document positive impacts only for several hundred people. Why?

I remember sitting with Mark Cabaj and asking some very difficult questions. It was obvious that we were doing the work we had set out to do. We were doing "things right" by engaging leaders, developing collective strategies, and working in teams. And yet it was just as obvious that we were not doing the "right things," as we were not getting the population-level changes we anticipated. We were not achieving the breakthrough community change we planned. We needed to change our approach.

We started by talking to everyone involved and asking where they observed the possibility of a breakthrough that would result in large-scale change. We clarified our desired outcome. In our case, it was that our work would reduce poverty rather than alleviate it. After selecting the strategies with the most promise, we followed these ideas carefully and built deep relationships with key actors. At the time, we called this "entering into the idea so we could gain a corner on the obvious."

Our approach worked. First, we focused on the human resource departments of public and private employers and asked them to audit their workplaces to determine if salary levels and working conditions contributed to people living in poverty. We encouraged them not only to pay better wages but also to develop policies that promote career advancement, better working conditions, and training. Second, we raised several million dollars that provided funding to community-based organizations so they could better innovate and implement "that one idea" they just knew would reduce poverty but could not find funding for. Third, we focused on the idea of policy change and asked the local government, employers, and training institutions to change their approach to providing services in a way that would either reduce costs or minimize barriers so low-income people would have more money in their pockets. As we saw promise and achieved buy-in for the emerging ideas, we adjusted our asks and scaled the ideas that were working. We achieved remarkable results.

By adjusting our strategy and focusing on three key initiatives, we started to see much better outcomes. We found our breakthrough. The work of social innovation requires constant learning and the willingness to adjust your approach and ways of thinking when needed.

Six Leadership Mindsets

I suggest that the attitude or approach you bring to the work of large-scale social change is extremely important. In this section I share six leadership mindsets that have helped me approach the work and lead to achieving impact.

1. Emergence Thinking

How do you know if you are doing the right things? You don't. Well, not at first, anyway. Most often, when you create a common agenda, you gain a good sense of the problem. You gain a more holistic understanding of the issues you want to resolve because you have engaged people with diverse life experiences. With this new understanding, you develop a vision and a handful of strategic directions. In theory, everything you write makes sense.

Then you move toward implementation. Each Work Team develops some form of an action plan that, in theory, makes sense. Next, you start to implement the action plan and if you are lucky, you get some early results. If you are super-lucky, you get amazing results. More likely, if your experience is like ours in the previous story, you will get some early outcomes, and then your impact stalls. At this point, you either abandon your approach or seek a different direction.

If you abandon your approach, you will need to start over. You ask, "Was the entire strategy direction wrong, or was it our action plan?" Before you answer this question, consider an emergent mindset.

An emergent mindset for implementing a strategy is to:

- Recognize that you are entering into the work to test your ideas and the approach. You are here to learn by doing, observing, reflecting, and then adjusting.

- Wait to see what emerges and what you are learning. Make changes and observe again. Reflect on this learning with the people who are the recipients of the actions as they are living the experience. Reflect with those who developed the approach, as their collective wisdom is powerful.

- Adjust. You can adjust incrementally and observe again. Then adjust boldly and observe again. You keep doing this while seeking ways to adjust your work toward larger-scale impacts.

- Push. When you start to see new patterns or levers of change emerging, push hard to harvest the outcomes.

Emergence thinking requires you to approach the work you are doing by looking for the reactions and interactions created. You are learning forward and seeking an impact. When you approach impact as a learner, you are in a sense peeling back the various layers of the problem, and over time the solution will be revealed.

2. Comprehensive Community Change Thinking

To achieve a breakthrough community change implies a whole community change. You are working toward an integrated network of programs and services. You seek to change many interrelated factors at the same time. We call this *comprehensive community change*. A comprehensive change mindset recognizes that the quality of life in a community is interdependent and requires a network of organizations working together to produce opportunities for personal safety, healthy lifestyle choices, economic security, learning, recreation, and relaxation. Feeling safe improves your quality of life, but if you are safe and do not have a source of income or access to health care or you cannot afford to learn, your overall quality of life is compromised.

When you think of your action plan through this same comprehensive lens, you open the door to discovering a pathway that will lead to large-scale change. Consider these questions: What are the interconnected factors in the work? When does acting in unison achieve a better outcome?

A forest is a great example of interconnected factors acting in unison to achieve the desired outcome of a healthy ecosystem. Can the trees be healthy if the streams are polluted? Can the animals be healthy if the plants are unhealthy? Like a forest, a healthy community requires multiple factors to be healthy simultaneously. Therefore, the solution required must seek multiple outcomes if you want breakthrough community change.

It is also important to understand that one person or one group doesn't have to do all the work; rather, comprehensive community change builds on the good work that is being led by multiple different groups, organizations, and levels of government. It's important to understand the scope of work that is being done and where the gaps might be, and to collaboratively set priorities for short-, mid-, and long-term action. This prevents the scope from being overwhelming and unmanageable. Multiple outcomes can emerge from multiple different sources, as long as all are working toward the common agenda.

3. Collective Innovation Thinking

Large-scale change assumes innovation. At the root of community, innovation is a good idea that a group of people work on together. This is not just any good idea, but rather an idea that achieves the desired outcome and improves the community. The closer we get to the "problem" we hope to affect, the easier it is to identify the assets of those experiencing the problem—those with lived experience. The better we understand how to harness community assets, the greater the probability that we will find the system-level changes needed to solve the problem. Evoking innovation is the ability of a collective group of people to grow the will of a community to change and then sustain that will. This is how breakthroughs occur.

A collective or collaborative innovation mindset is most important for solving human challenges. The day a child is born, a community is transformed. People become parents, the parents of the new parents become grandparents, siblings of the new parents become aunts and uncles, and so on. This child transforms all the relationships of the parents and the context (neighborhood, schools, etc.) in which they coexist is engaged differently. A new idea or approach needs to transform a network of relationships so that people act differently. The idea itself might be innovative, but as it matures, relationships change. When relationships change toward the new desired outcome, the impact we hope for emerges.

A community innovation mindset achieves the desired long-term sustainable impact and reframes how people see themselves in the context of the issue. This is the essential role that community innovation needs to play in community change.

4. Policy Change Thinking

Ultimately, breakthrough community change works to change the policies that have caused the problem in the first place. Breakthrough community change creates better policies that will truly address the problem. In government, we have policies that will ensure social well-being. Schools have policies for what teachers should teach and how they should teach it. Business has policies for how they should treat their employees and how employees should treat each other. In the simplest terms, community policies are the agreed-upon rules or conditions that allow the group to live in a community together. These may also be referred to as *principles of action*.

Sometimes policy can be changed by a small group of people that recommend a change in the wording or the intent of an existing policy. Sometimes people actively protest a policy (think apartheid), and change occurs when the power structures benefiting from that policy relent. The best way for a policy to change is when most people agree that it is in their best interest and they begin to act differently. The policy is purely a reflection of majority agreement.

In breakthrough community change, we want to create the momentum for whole system change. In other words, we want people to act differently at such a scale that the policy makers start to write new policies or change the old ones because they seem irrelevant. In Calgary, a group of activists was protesting the cost of transportation. The city had just raised the cost of public transit and many people felt that transit fares were out of reach for people living on a low income. At first, the protest was brought to city council meetings in the form of delegations. When the city council would not budge, the protest took to the streets and escalated to the point where protesters were lying down in front of buses or hosting sit-ins on public transit. Still, the city council would not budge and called in the police to deal with what they considered disruptive behavior.

Vibrant Communities Calgary (VCC) is a collaboration of business leaders, government, community organizations, and people with lived/living experiences of poverty. They were exploring options for reducing poverty together. In the early stages of their work, they stumbled across an important possibility for change. They approached the group of transit fare protestors to understand what needed to change for them to believe things might improve. At first, the protesters demanded free transportation for everyone. VCC used this as a base for understanding how free transportation would improve the lives of many people. Essentially, reliable and affordable transit would give low-income people the mobility necessary to live a better life, including getting themselves to and from their jobs and their children to and from school.

What was important is that VCC had prominent business leaders, senior administrators, and politicians active in their collaborative. These individuals saw the reasoning behind the protest. They began to see that there might be a solution that would be better for everyone in Calgary. There were many meetings and discussions. In less than three months, an agreement was reached. The city offered a 50 percent discount on all transit passes for people living on or below the official poverty line. This was to become the new policy. As a result of the negotiation, thousands of Calgarians had affordable transportation—not a perfect solution, but one that worked for everyone. Every person living in poverty and using public transit would have the extra money in their pockets.

A policy change mindset is required for all breakthrough community change. The principles of action reflected in a policy change only when people see reason in the change and agree to act differently. The work of the community collaboration seeking systems change is to find those ideas that are at the root of the issue addressed. These ideas can be identified as constraints. Our goal is first to raise the importance of the constraints, and second to engage many people in discussions that lead to improved understanding. Third, we need to find a better alternative that is widely agreed upon by all sectors in our collaborative. Fourth, we need to propose this change in a strategic way that makes it easy for policy makers to change their policy. Of course, if only it were that easy! The power of a collaborative is the network of relationships and the ability of a diverse group of people to agree and compromise.

5. "Everyone Changes Just a Little Bit" Thinking

Being focused on your community plan is critical to your success—especially if you enter the work through an emergent mindset, constantly adjusting while looking for ways the community can innovate, and address policies to realize an impact. Your actions will cause broader commitment to your goal and you will be creating the conditions for large-scale change. Be focused, but never discourage the broader changes you are inspiring and evoking from those who are observing you: your supporters.

Our experience is that by continually encouraging your partners to make their own changes, you can inspire many actions that are not directly captured in your strategies. An employer starts to pay better wages. A city council changes the costs of use of facilities and permits, and community programs become more resilient. Our work is to encourage everyone to change just a little. It is exactly these "thousand flowers blooming" that embody the essence of whole community change. As a collaborative, you created the conditions for the community to change. People get a sense that your campaign is working, and they want to be part of that change.

When you join together, a common hope for a better community emerges. Then little changes occur. Everyone is involved and change starts to spread. When this hope feels real, it inspires people to change, if even just a little bit. A CEO declares they are paying everyone in their company no less than $15 an hour even though the minimum wage is $10 an hour. A single mother living in poverty applies to go back to school because she believes a better future is possible. A person of wealth comes forward with a large donation to your work. The mayor approaches your group and asks, "How can I help?"

This is the change that is seldom spoken about. Breakthrough community change happens when we act together. We hope for significant change. Our entire community is inspired to believe that this hope is possible, and they are willing to change and contribute.

6. "Getting to Maybe" Thinking

Breakthrough change is an ambition. It is not a guarantee. My favorite book about social change is *Getting to Maybe: How the World Is Changed* by Frances Westley, Brenda Zimmerman, and Michael Quinn Patton.[1] The book is about social innovation and social innovators. It helped me to accept a new paradigm for social change. We often assume that new social change ideas will succeed. *Getting to Maybe* provides a much better context for social change. We embark on new change ideas with the assurance that we tried, and, hopefully, we did our best to do what we thought was necessary. The big outcomes we hoped for are never assured. This does not make the idea or the effort any less important. This kind of social change work matters. The effort is worth it, whether we succeed or not.

Conclusion

This chapter is full of high-level ideas that could each warrant a book. I share them knowing that they may be more advanced than you might need if you are just getting started. I do, though, want you to know that people are thinking about these approaches. When your impact is stalled and the work is challenging, these ideas are available for you to consider.

8
Understanding Impact

*Collecting data and measuring results consistently on
a shortlist of indicators at the community level and
across all participating organizations not only ensures
that all efforts remain aligned, but it also enables the
participants to hold each other accountable and learn
from each other's successes and failures.*

—JOHN KANIA AND MARK KRAMER

A GUIDE TO:

- Understanding feedback systems
- Tracking contributions
- Deciding what to measure and how to measure it
- Creating evaluations that are useful, collaborative, empowering, and responsive
- Understanding shared measurement

NO MATTER HOW HARD WE work or how disciplined or smart our delivery is, if we are working at
a strategy that is not achieving the right outcomes, we will

not achieve a breakthrough that might lead to large-scale change.

Asking broader questions, measuring, and observing outcomes for the change we want to see are critical to having a strong impact. The ways we measure our impact should inform the adaptation of strategy rather than holding a group accountable to a rigid plan. To inform adaptation we need reality testing and feedback loops. Progress should be tracked using contribution, not attribution. The evaluation process should be designed and carried out in ways that empower stakeholders and organized around their questions.

I remember the first letter that was being sent out by Tamarack and the McConnell Family Foundation to our trail builders in our national program to support cities to end poverty. These groups would work for a year engaging their communities and together build a community plan. They submitted that plan to our team for both financial and coaching support valued at nearly $1 million. This letter— signed by Tim Brodhead, CEO of the foundation—congratulated them for their exemplary efforts and on being awarded this contribution toward their work.

The letter included a statement that Tim insisted upon. "Congratulations on your exceptional plan. We are, though, not funding you to implement this plan. If you implement this exact plan, we will be disappointed. We are funding you because we are so impressed by the process you have undertaken to engage your community and for the collective wisdom that has produced. We want this learning and community engagement to continue, and we are excited by how much more you will learn once you implement your plan. We fully expect you to change and adapt." Our community partners were both delighted and confused by this statement.

The Importance of Getting the Right Feedback and Adapting

The key to getting to impact is to learn and adapt as you move toward your goal. Learning together as a community provides the opportunity to better understand the issue being addressed and the possible solutions to deploy. To learn collectively, you need both single- and double-loop feedback systems.

A single-loop feedback system is a series of approaches that helps us understand if we are *doing things right*. Understanding if we are doing things the right way is helpful but inadequate if we want to learn how to achieve the target outcomes. For that, we need to add double-loop feedback, which helps us understand if we are *doing the right things*. Are people living better lives because of our work? What are we learning that will move us toward our desired change? Are any policies being changed? What significant systems have been affected? Both single-loop and double-loop feedback are a necessary tension in any successful venture.

We need to ask, "Who cares about our work?" We then need to ask those who care, "What questions do you have about our work that you would like us to answer in this evaluation?" These questions are central to creating a feedback system. When the questions are grouped and prioritized, they orient the focus of the evaluation. This is simple. I would say the obvious idea of asking those who care what they want to learn is ideally suited for reviewing the impacts of a breakthrough community change initiative. It provides an approach in which all stakeholders can shape the evaluation. Stakeholders can be engaged in the outcomes or learnings from the evaluation. This strengthens the community's commitment to collaborative work and facilitates learning and changing together.

Stakeholders must meet regularly to discuss their collaborative community change. A common agenda has the potential to change everything when a whole community contributes toward the impact you hope to achieve. In Des Moines, Iowa, Opportunities Central Iowa convenes their collaborative every quarter. They use these gatherings to learn together, discuss progress, and brainstorm ideas to advance their impact. In Maine, the Maine Cancer Foundation convenes its partners every year for an entire day of learning and inspiration and to review their collective work.

These community conversations are ongoing. The process is a container that holds a place for a natural and continuous cycle of thinking, planning, and doing. These are the forums where a collaborative can adapt and change course.

Tracking Contribution vs. Attribution

A major mindset shift is required to understand the impact of whole community change. We need to shift our thinking away from attribution to contribution.

Attribution thinking is used to determine the extent to which the changes that emerge in a community are attributable to the activities of the would-be changemakers or some other non-intervention factors. This approach, though useful in evaluating the effects of a specific intervention, limits our analysis and draws us away from the multiple factors or contributions that realized the change.[1]

Contribution thinking acknowledges multiple factors that underlie an observed change and seeks to understand the contribution of the community or collective effort activities. The idea behind contribution thinking is to simply acknowledge that the named intervention is only one of many factors behind a community change and that our objective is to assess the relative contribution of the intervention.[2]

Contribution thinking can positively affect our progress to whole community change in the following ways:

- Contribution thinking encourages us to seek out multiple contributors toward a specific outcome. This is important in community change since it fosters a culture of cooperation rather than competition. When we seek to attribute an outcome specifically to our work, we become more concerned about how our specific effort created an intended result. With contribution thinking, we consider the intended result and then consider the various organizations that worked together to enable this outcome.

- Contribution thinking urges us to consider the multiple factors that result in an outcome. In large-scale change very few issues that matter have simple causes. When we accept that a comprehensive approach to change is required, we can recognize the multiple interventions that exist in a community to address this, and we seek to share how each intervention is contributing to better outcomes.

- Contribution thinking provides a lens into the whole system of support and leads us to identify the gap in service that requires bridging to be more effective. In this way, we can link programs and services so that they are working more effectively.

- Contribution thinking moves funders to think holistically and ask: How does this project we are funding contribute to the overall well-being of the community? How is it improving the broader outcomes we are hoping for?

What Do We Measure?

Though I feel we need to be flexible and constantly adapting, I have adopted several principles for tracking change and outcomes. These are markers or footholds to ensure that the change is real.

I like to track three equally important outcomes. Any one of these three outcomes measured alone will not tell the full story of breakthrough change, but together they provide an excellent starting point.

Outcome 1:
Measuring Changes in Individuals' Lives

We need to identify real improvements in people's lives. We need to be able to describe how people are living better lives because of our work. We need to be able to quantify how many people have improved life situations because of our work. If we are solving working poverty, we need to identify how many people have moved out of working poverty. If our goal is to reduce cancer rates, then we need to track the reduction in people with cancer in our community. If we want to improve the mental health of young people, we need to track how many young people have improved mental health.

Outcome 2:
Measuring Changes in Community Learning

We want to identify what we are learning together as a community and what change has resulted because of our learning. We might ask: How is our community learning together about the issue we are addressing? What changes in behaviors are occurring as a result? When we learn that working poverty is not only about wages but also about the number of hours worked in a year, we want to document how this new information impacts our action plan.

Outcome 3:
Measuring Changes in Policies and Systems

We want to identify the policy or system changes that are influenced by our work. Has an employer changed its hiring practices? Has the municipality or city committed to eliminating working poverty within its workforce?

I know that we can identify many other impacts that occur during our work. I am convinced that if our work does not result in real people living better lives, our community has not learned or changed together. If no policies are created or changed, then we are not doing the right things and we will not achieve a breakthrough that results in a large-scale change.

Evaluations

Evaluation is often required by funders. Evaluators often struggle to identify the kinds of evaluation that can be used in community change processes. My experience is that traditional formative and summative forms of evaluation can lead to very difficult and seldom useful conversations. Most groups embarking on a community change process feel misunderstood by traditional evaluators, who are not experienced in participatory forms of evaluation. There are several important principles I want to consider when evaluating a collaborative community-wide initiative.

Evaluations Should Be Useful

Evaluations can be tools for growth and improvement, or they can be used to negatively impact the program. And, of course, evaluations can be placed on shelves to become dust collectors. When we evaluate because our funder or boss tells us to do so, the evaluation does nothing to help our work. Evaluations are also used to serve other groups' or funders' purposes—perhaps to prove that they need more staff or that a partner or funder is being unreasonable. This use of evaluation may be helpful, but it's seldom useful in your community change efforts. My experience is that people ignore or misuse evaluations because they do not feel involved or engaged, or, worse, they feel judged by an evaluation.

There are more effective and affirming ways to use evaluations. Evaluations can be used to generate new insights and understanding about the issue being addressed. Key insights from clients or partners can provide valuable information to move the group closer to the community issue addressed. Evaluations can also be used to uncover process improvements that can result in adaptations and modifications to the work. Useful evaluations can complement the development process and provide insight that supports more efficient processes and better outcomes. A useful evaluation can help your group understand how to achieve the breakthrough you desire.

Evaluations Should Be Responsive

Three principles are central to the process of designing an evaluation plan that is responsive to your community change partners.

First, an evaluation should be designed so that community partners and people with lived experience decide on the questions being explored and are included in designing the process used in the evaluation. That does not mean that the evaluator does not bring their expertise to the conversation. It does mean that there is a discussion about the process and joint agreement among the evaluator, community partners, and those with lived experience of the issue at hand.

Second, the work of sensemaking is a shared goal between the community and the evaluator. We want to engage in questions that enhance our collective understanding of the community change story we have embarked on together.

Third, we answer the questions, "So what?" and "Now what?" There is agreement that we discuss the relevance of our findings and that we will jointly agree on the action items identified in the evaluation.

Evaluations Should Empower

Most importantly, we want the evaluation process to empower people and give voice to those who often are not included. To better understand the impact at a community change level, we want a process of evaluation that provides the opportunity for our partners to ask the questions that need to be asked. When the questions being asked are meaningful to participants, there is community ownership. We also want a process that builds community capacity. We want people to learn from evaluations by ensuring the possible answers to questions they helped to formulate are discussed. This ensures they are engaged.

Shared Measurement Data

The Leadership Team wanted systems change and they needed to understand what was happening at a population level. They hoped that with a better understanding of the data, they might be able to use it to educate and debate with community changemakers about the data and the kind of change that was needed. They also wanted to help their community to better use data in decision-making. Over time, the community was able to identify and agree on using several key outcome measures tracked consistently as one of their shared measurements of impact.

Shared measurement is one of the five key conditions of collective impact. It helps us to tell a story and understand the picture of change, what is working and what is not. Shared measurement helps to identify the effectiveness and ineffectiveness of our strategies. As John Kania and Mark Kramer share in their seminal paper on collective impact, "Collecting data and measuring results consistently on a short list of indicators at the community level and across all participating organizations not only ensures that all efforts remain aligned, but it also enables the participants to hold each other accountable and learn from each other's successes and failures."[3]

Shared measurement supports organizations to align their efforts around shared outcomes, track and evaluate their collective progress, and benchmark results. Most importantly, it positions organizations to learn from each other about the kind of data that matters to them in making decisions. As a community works collectively to understand the data required to make better decisions, a shared measurement approach improves the quality and credibility of data available. When communities work together to find data needs they have in common, they can access this data collectively to reduce the costs of collecting and reporting on it.

Shared measurement is about identifying common metrics for tracking progress toward a common agenda across multiple organizations. Shared measurement provides scalable platforms to share data, discuss learnings, and improve strategies and actions. It allows for a cohesive approach to sense-making and for a process that can inform practice, activities, and actions and connect with outcomes. Shared measures are best established once a common agenda has been developed.

Breakthrough community change requires us to adopt contribution thinking and to consider ways that we can measure the contribution of multiple actors and the effectiveness of multiple interventions. This is where we can begin to see how the whole is greater than the individual parts.

9
Renewing or Winding Down

Those who struggle to make a difference have to face two paradoxes. The first is that success is not a fixed address. The second is that failure can open the way to success.

—FRANCES WESTLEY, BRENDA ZIMMERMAN,
AND MICHAEL QUINN PATTON

A GUIDE TO:

- Understanding what happens when the campaign nears the end of its time frame
- Deciding to renew or wind down the campaign
- Engaging the community in making the decision

IN CHAPTER 5 I SHARED why I like to organize the breakthrough community change implementation phase as a campaign. A campaign allows us to establish targets that motivate people. This builds momentum and excitement about the goals. It helps people to push hard. It allows you to develop a time-limited plan of either three or five years. Campaigns using this approach do end, and we must consider sustaining the work through a renewal process or winding it down.

In the first breakthrough community change campaign I led, we established a goal to reduce poverty in the Waterloo Region to the lowest level in Canada by the year 2000. It was marketed as our region's "gift" for a better world, as we were moving into a new millennium. Our five-year campaign was to run from the beginning of 1996 to the end of 2000. We called the campaign Opportunities 2000. Our simple goal was to reduce overall poverty by two thousand families, which would effectively make the Region of Waterloo the region with the lowest level of poverty in Canada.

The campaign had very specific numerical goals and a defined time period to accomplish them. We assumed that at the end of 2000, we would wind down our campaign and declare our results. At the defined date, we were four hundred families short of our goal but had some projects that were still operating. We predicted that within a year these projects, when completed, would help us meet our target. So we extended the campaign by one year, fully anticipating an end date. The year was also a transition year to determine if the campaign would continue or wind down. In Opportunities 2000 there was tremendous pressure to keep our efforts going. People wanted to end poverty, and many believed that if the campaign were continued, we might achieve this.

Engaging Your Community to Decide

Declaring an end date for a campaign is not without risks. Looking five years into the future, we can make some ambitious projections that will be hard to achieve. A more conservative approach is to launch an initial three-year plan with the renewal as an action item in year three of your plan. My experience is that it is harder to achieve breakthrough community change in a three-year program. Yet if your group is deliberate about building and sustaining momentum, this approach can work.

As you decide whether you should renew your campaign or wind it down, the following questions will prove useful:

- Are there leaders within your current campaign that are committed to staying for at least two or three years if you renew? If you cannot receive a renewal commitment from key leaders, then you should consider winding down. If you do receive such commitment, these leaders should play a significant role in the renewal.

- Ask your community if you should renew or wind down. Hosting a full-day community conversation can help you gauge community will and energy for a second campaign. Ensure that this is a multisector conversation that includes government, business, community, and lived/living experience leaders. Ensure your funders attend this gathering.

- Ask who are the strongest advocates for renewal. When funders are encouraging you to continue, it is extremely difficult to be objective. Is the desire for renewal funder-driven or community-driven?

- What have you accomplished in the first campaign? Will more time produce significant impacts? Will renewal sustain high-impact initiatives or realize the full outcome of a significant policy change?

- Consider alternatives to renewal. Are there community partners who would take on a specific aspect of your work? Are these initiatives better sustained by that community partner?

Deciding to renew or wind down will never be an easy decision. How does one end a project that is having a major impact? It is important to remember that you need your community to join you if you are going to continue, so taking the time to listen is paramount.

Reasons for Campaign Wind-Down

People get attached to programs that produce positive outcomes. There is a definite desire to keep going. So often I hear, "Why would we end something so successful?" I have observed campaigns end with great success. The key to a proper wind-down is to be deliberate and to engage your full community in the decision.

I suggest three reasons to wind down a breakthrough community change project at the defined end date of a campaign:

- A time-defined campaign motivates people and is highly effective in sustaining momentum. If you are going to use a campaign approach with integrity, then ending it when you said you would is the right thing to do. People worked hard and stuck with the work. There is a general feeling of accomplishment when things end. By being deliberate you can wind the work down proudly and properly.

- By ending a campaign, you create room for another community-wide campaign. The ending of a campaign can cause a void and open a space for another major issue to be addressed.

- Momentum is hard to maintain beyond five years, and the work it takes to renew and rebuild is difficult to achieve. If you are lucky, many of the leaders active in your campaign remained active for the entire five-year period. Finding new leadership can be difficult.

To wind down a campaign requires time and patience. There will be many opinions. I suggest you start this conversation a year before you make the final decision. You should build transition time into your budget planning as well so the decision to end does not happen because you ran out of money. Most importantly, if you wind down, ensure you throw a huge party where people are thanked and your accomplishment and efforts are celebrated.

Reasons and Tips for a Campaign Renewal

I have observed dozens of breakthrough community change campaigns that have continued after the scheduled campaign end date. There are so many important reasons for renewing a campaign. Change takes time. Here are some reasons and a few tips for success if you are considering a continuation:

- It is important to end your initial campaign properly— to celebrate, to share gratitude with those who have made significant impacts (I like award ceremonies), and to tell the story of the campaign. Let the momentum end momentarily to celebrate and take stock.

- People can be very resilient when they believe they are part of something that is truly changing their community. I also suggest that you create a clear "ask" for people that allows them to exit or stay on. I suggest that a successful campaign renewal have a minimum 50 percent change in leadership. In most cases, this also applies to the staff team.

- I suggest a one-year gap, a gap year, in which you celebrate and then rebuild momentum. I suggest that you use a similar process that you used to launch the first campaign. Form a Leadership Roundtable with the task of developing a second campaign. Form a Listening Team that will host many community conversations to determine the most compelling actions required to establish your next strategy. Form a Data Team to deeply understand the numerical case for change. Develop Action Teams to test new ideas and approaches. You can continue some of the projects that are still generating outcomes. Key leaders with a real passion for this work can continue.

- To continue, you must make sure that funders are still on board. Most campaign funding is structured around the length of the campaign. Involving your funders in the renewal process is critical. Good funder stewardship practices are always important, but remember that the more you involve the funders throughout your campaign, the more likely they will continue to fund you should you decide to continue.

- This is obvious but still important to mention: you are not starting over. You are building on the work you have done over the full length of your campaign. Most likely you have a great reputation in the community, a history of collaboration on the issue, and highly supportive community leadership and funders. The issue is still very important to the community. These points all have to be considered when you ask your community about continuing.

I recently supported a group that renewed their campaign as a ten-year strategy. It was bolder than their previous five-year strategy and declared that ending poverty was a generational ambition. This approach worked, and with a strategic renewal plan, they managed the transition very well. I believe that they adhered to all five of the preceding tips.

Whether you wind down or sustain through a renewal process, know that the work you started and the impact you have had on your community will last for many years. Your community has experienced an advanced form of collaboration. People have learned to work across sectors and most specifically with people who have lived experiences of the issue. My experience is that the stronger the history of collaboration in a community, the easier and more effective subsequent collaborative efforts are. Knowing that you have contributed to building the collaborative knowledge and experience for your community will produce many more collaboration change initiatives and bold outcomes for several generations.

10
What's Next?

"be careful what you wish for,
it might come true."
Maybe that's exactly why
there are so many of them—
the universe gives us extra chances
to keep dreaming.
Each one an uprising,
a burst of color
in the cracks of our hearts,
sunrise
at an unexpected time,
an unexpected place.

FROM "LUCIEN'S BIRTHDAY POEM"
BY ELLIE SCHOENFELD (USED WITH PERMISSION)

A GUIDE TO:

- Identifying your starting point
- Focusing on your True North
- Finding the inspiration needed to do more

WHAT'S NEXT FOR YOU AS you consider the sequence of ideas shared in this book?

As you consider if you are ready for the work of breakthrough community change, can you describe an aha moment that is transforming old ways of thinking, reinvigorating energies, and leading you to a new, more innovative way of living? The power of the personal breakthrough can be harnessed to increase community engagement, identify community assets, work collaboratively to build a common agenda, and implement a large-scale community plan.

Has your journey as a team that has experienced breakthroughs stimulated your efforts and energies to reach your goals? Are you ready for more?

Where to Start?

David Brooks, one of America's most famous columnists, wrote an article in the *New York Times* in April 2019 about Tamarack's work and the Vibrant Communities network of cities across Canada working to end poverty. I met David when he attended a conference in which I was presenting a workshop with long-time collaborators Tim Brodhead, former CEO of the McConnell Family Foundation, and Elisabeth Buck, former CEO of the Central Iowa United Way. David spontaneously showed up at one of the workshops we were presenting and later asked if he could write an article about our work. His article is summarized below. His words inspired many people. What inspired me most is that he answered the question of "Now what?" in such a precise way, as if he wanted to answer the question: Where do we start if we want large-scale community change?

I encourage you to use these six ideas from his article as a wonderful summary of a "Now what?" map for your journey.[1]

They adopted a specific methodology . . . So, they began building citywide and communitywide structures.

They begin by gathering, say, 100 people from a single community. A quarter have lived in poverty; the rest are from business, non-profits, and governments.

They spend a year learning . . . and talking with the community. They launch a different kind of conversation . . . they up their ambitions . . . they broaden their vision.

After a year they come up with a town plan. . . . Each town's assets are different. So each town's plan is different.

The plans involve a lot of policy changes on the town and provincial (and national) levels.

[The Tamarack Institute] emphasizes that the crucial thing these communitywide collective impact structures do is change attitudes. In the beginning, it's as if everybody is swimming in polluted water. People are sluggish, fearful, isolated, and looking out only for themselves. But when people start working together across sectors around a common agenda, it's like cleaning the water.

I love the sequence David Brooks used to describe our work. He highlights the need for a methodology, the central role of engagement, and the time it takes to think and unthink the issue as a community. He emphasizes that cities and communities are all different and that they need their own approach to planning—that it takes time. The fact is that we cannot get the kind of breakthrough changes we desire unless we have key system players involved. This includes local, state, or national governments and other major employers who are willing to make some policy changes.

His final paragraph inspired me the most. The idea of refreshing "the water" was a new breakthrough for me. *People were no longer sluggish; they were energized, and they could see the change they wanted now.*

Creating a common agenda can change everything or, as Brooks writes, "when people start working together across sectors around a common agenda, it's like cleaning the water."

Your True North

As you continue to explore your approach and the required skill sets you need to achieve a breakthrough, I ask that you consider the following three key ideas as a compass that will keep you moving in the right direction on your journey toward community change.

First, breakthrough community change ensures that everyone that can affect a problem is involved in solving it.

Second, breakthrough community change requires that working together at the community level happens frequently. Business, government, and nonprofit sectors should be planning together with the people most affected by the problem: those who have lived or are living at the center of the issue addressed. It requires that we have joint community-wide plans and systems in place that track collective outcomes.

Third, breakthrough community change ensures that we focus on population outcomes and see them as primary values. We need to be able to communicate how our collective actions are affecting our community. We need to share how our lives are better because we are working together.

Words of Encouragement

There are days when it is hard to be hopeful. As we see news of environmental change and we listen to politicians who spread hate and division, our hearts sink. Organizations can become entrenched and people fearful. The positive change we long for can so easily dissipate.

I ask that you have the courage and take the time to see past the challenges. Look into the hearts and ambitions of the people who live around you. I have met and worked with thousands of people to build better cities and communities. I have found we all have three things in common. We want to live in a safe and nurturing place. We want greater opportunities for ourselves and our children. We want to live in an equitable and democratic world. My experience is that even if people have vastly different political approaches, faith-based beliefs, or cultural understandings, we are far more the same than we are different. I have come to see that we don't all need to believe in the same things to work well to build a great city. We just need to care about the same things. Fundamentally, we do.

Now what? What we need is the opportunity to meet each other, have a conversation from the heart, and embrace each other's stories. Never fear people's desire to organize, says Margaret Wheatley: "They always will." The real issue is: Will they organize against one another or with each other? I believe that if we can equip people with solid principles and collaborative practices, they will organize with each other. They will find space for their ideas and bring their best to the common table.

Community change is possible. All you need is a breakthrough!

PART II

Skill Sets for Community Change

P ART II DESCRIBES THE SKILLS and knowledge that will support the most effective implementation of the methodology described in Part I. The six skill sets are associated with the following community change approaches:

- Asset-based community development
- Collective impact
- Community engagement
- Community innovation
- Collaborative leadership
- Community change evaluation

Each community change approach I share is to act as a reference guide or a road map for further study. As you read through Part II, certain skills and knowledge will be familiar to you. You will probably be able to identify how you are using or have used those skills throughout your journey. I like to encourage people to start with their strengths and work from there. Each chapter in Part II contains a list of resources for further learning. These are a few books and authors I want to share with you who are important references as you deepen your learning.

Beyond reflecting on your personal level of the skills and knowledge described, I encourage you to begin to identify the individuals in your community who have honed their skills in and developed their knowledge of the various community change approaches I have highlighted. These are the people you want to recruit for your network and leadership roles. Building your collaboration to achieve breakthrough community change is easier and more efficient when the team has strong skills and depth of knowledge.

You can refer to the descriptions of the skills and knowledge as often as you like while you are doing your work. They will remind you of the core skills required and the knowledge-based principles that are relevant to achieving the kind of breakthrough change you are seeking.

11
Connecting the Dots: Six Skill Sets for Community Change

Give people good information and effective tools, and they will organize and work together to create the kind of communities they want.

—DAVID CHRISLIP

A GUIDE TO:

- Developing key skills for community change
- Implementing six important frameworks for community change
- Learning how the six frameworks are more powerful when enacted together

---

THE PROCESS FOR BREAKTHROUGH community change is only part of the journey. The most effective community changemakers have a developing awareness of and knowledge of theories and concepts around how communities function, how policies are developed, and how people are engaged in the process of change. Population-level transformation is complex and draws from valuable information found in asset-based community development, collective impact, community engagement, community innovation, collaborative leadership, and community change evaluation. There are six approaches of skills and knowledge for break-through community change. New and updated research on these ideas and strategies continues to emerge as this book is being published. Part II of this book provides more detailed descriptions of these ideas, skills, tools, and strategies for you to build a strong foundation for the process described in Part I.

In writing my master's thesis, I was exploring the ideas and skill sets of collaborative leadership. I titled the thesis *Leaderful Communities* and described the work of many leaders doing brilliant work individually through the organizations they ran and then agreeing to work together, not as a homogenous group but as gifted leaders with unique skill sets, well-developed knowledge, and independent visions.[1] They united through a common agenda to each contribute to the good of the whole. I named these leaderful communities because I observed many leaders coexisting and each bringing their best to a common agenda.

The skills associated with the community change approaches can be simple skills that we use to be more efficient as we complete tasks. The skills are built on the knowledge about the approaches and can be applied as we make big ideas practical. The skills can be functions or principles we use to define our work. Most importantly, skills can be rehearsed and improved.

Both skills and knowledge can be owned by an individual and combined with the talents and understanding of a team, group, or community. Communities require diverse skills and a depth of knowledge so they can collaborate, innovate, take on challenges, and create opportunities together.

In community change, the skills of individuals collaborating create a synergistic whole. While each is strong in its own right, the six community change approaches are most effective when changemakers are comfortable with and knowledgeable about all of the skill sets associated with them so that they can draw upon each and combine them as needed to advance the team's agenda toward breakthrough community change.

Somewhat like an orchestra.

I was talking with a friend who is a musician. He described something he read online about the beautiful process of how a collection of unique instruments, when played together, maintains the integrity of each individual sound and yet also creates a unified whole that is greater than any one instrument can make at the same time and still be distinctly recognizable.

Every instrument produces a different sound because of the sound wave created when it is played. The sound wave of a flute is simple because the sound is created by air vibrating along a cylindrical tube. The sound wave of a violin is more complex. It is made up of the vibration of the strings, created when they are bowed or plucked. The sound moves into the air of the violin's body and vibrates around inside it before being reflected in the air outside the instrument. It makes a very different sound wave than the flute.

Other instruments produce their sounds in different ways. In a piano, a hammer hits a string. In the viola, cello, and bass, the bodies of the instruments and length of the strings are different from the violin, which makes their sound similar but respectively deeper.

In other wind instruments, the sound is created in different ways, using a single reed (clarinets and saxophones), double reeds (oboe, English horn, and bassoon), and lips vibrating in brass instruments (horns, trumpets, trombones, and tubas). They travel down tubes of different shapes. For example, compare the clarinet and sax. They both initially produce their sounds with the vibration of a single reed, but in a clarinet the sound travels down a uniform cylinder with a small bell opening, while in a sax, the tube is conical with a wider bell opening. These types of variations make the sounds different from each other. Each instrument has its own unique sound, and when played together as in an orchestra or jazz band, the competing yet collaborating sounds are unified into majestic music.

We can follow this same path as we collaborate with our community. We bring our unique talents, skills, and gifts to the work of the whole. Breakthrough community change is recognizing that we can do more together when we unite our community than any of us can do alone. By working toward a common agenda and a common approach, we bring the unique skills and assets of each individual into the process of change. When we become an interconnected force, large-scale breakthrough community change is possible. In other words, we can make beautiful music together.

The innovation that is part of genuine large-scale community change requires us to hold the knowledge and the skills of the six approaches in tandem. In so doing, we increase our likelihood of breakthrough community change and population-level impact.

Looking for a Breakthrough? Develop Your Skills. Expand Your Knowledge.

Breakthrough community change is built by taking the best knowledge and skills from six distinct yet complementary community change approaches. If you want to engage in the kind of community change that leads to breakthroughs,

I suggest that you become a student of all six approaches. The body of research on population-level and whole community change has been expanding over the past thirty years. There are multiple approaches to community change. These are six research-supported and well-developed approaches that I understand as essential in working toward a breakthrough community change.

When you are organizing for community change, I would hang out a metaphorical sign that reads, "Skilled Practitioners Welcome." It is well worth your time to look for people in your community that are skilled and or knowledgeable in asset-based community development, collective impact, community engagement, community innovation, collaborative leadership, and community change evaluation. I hope that you use this opportunity to build these skills and the knowledge they represent by hosting learning circles and seminars in your community.

Asset-Based Community Development

Asset-based community development (ABCD) is rooted in the central idea that communities can act on their own to solve their most pressing challenges. Communities embrace the idea that the change they seek is best tackled by residents acting together as opposed to waiting for some outside force to change their circumstances. By moving from the mindset of change being "done *to*" to change being "done *with*," we fundamentally rethink our approach. ABCD starts with the premise that residents have gifts that they want to share and that harnessing these assets creates a powerful force for change, as opposed to the notion that a community is made up of various deficits and challenges that need to be overcome. ABCD skills include uniting people as a whole community, building relationships, and fostering ownership to build momentum for change. By involving everyone in the process of change, we create more equitable communities.

Collective Impact

Collective impact is a powerful set of ideas and strategies. A community united in a common agenda and acting together for breakthrough change requires good tools and processes to take the work to scale. Collective impact is the most advanced form of collaborative action currently available. The skills include building a common agenda and a shared measurement system, which make it easier for a community and its partners to work together, create opportunities, and strengthen mutually reinforcing activities. The skill of continuous communication keeps the partners aligned and builds momentum, while the backbone governance and staffing model provides an agreed-upon structure for action and dedicated professionals to support its implementation.

Community Engagement

Community engagement skill sets are extremely important because sustainable community change requires everyone in a community to be engaged, not just the traditional leaders and organizations associated with the issue. For large-scale change to occur, we need the skill to engage many people who believe in the cause and are willing to act. I have observed that people become committed and actively participate in the work of large-scale community change when they have good information, are consulted about the desired change, and have opportunities to be involved in the change process.

Community Innovation

Community innovation is a central concept of the breakthrough community change approach. To innovate, we must do more than work harder, smarter, or invest more money in the current way of doing things. Change at the community level requires skills that help us to rethink current systems of program delivery. It requires us to come up with new ideas. It requires us to be creative and think beyond the usual ways of doing things. It requires us to understand design thinking. It requires us to reach out across sectors. It requires us to reach out to people most affected by the issue we are trying to address.

Collaborative Leadership

Collaborative leadership is community change work on a personal level. It requires people involved in the change process to consider how they show up in the work. I often express collaborative leadership in this way: I am a leader, we are all leaders, there is work to do, let's get on with it. This provides an approach for building collective action. We can develop skills to recognize that leadership is an individual who desires change. When leaders become engaged, we deploy skills that help people take ownership of the change desired. Finally, we require skills to help leaders collectively engage and support them to join forces to create collaborative action.

Community Change Evaluation

At Tamarack, we frequently consider three levels of outcomes when we track community change. First, we require skills to track how many individuals and families have experienced an improvement in their lives because of the programs that have been put into place. Second, we need skills to track a community's potential by understanding and documenting how its capacity for change is improving. This involves learning to track outcomes such as expanded cross-sector collaboration, strengthened engagement with people of lived experience, or a more exact and broadly held understanding of the issue. Third, we want to develop skills to track large-scale sustainable change at the policy and systems level. Systems-level changes in approach to the issue on an organizational level or a community-wide level are tracked, as they are evidence of large-scale community change.

Participatory and collaborative forms of evaluation are essential skills for understanding the impact of breakthrough community change, as they recognize that collective change cannot scale unless we understand collaborative outcomes and approaches. A shared measurement system requires us to understand not only what we want to change, but also how we might be able to measure the change as real and tangible at the population level. The people who are acting together for change must be engaged to learn together. Their participation in the evaluation is critical to collective learning.

Connecting the Dots

It is so important for all contributors not only to *understand* their role in or contribution to the process, but also to feel comfortable with it, *embrace* it, and even take it one step further and *lead* with it. Roadblocks can happen when participants are confused about their role or contribution or fear taking something on.

Each approach is important. It is very helpful to have people in the network who have a deeper knowledge of the six approaches. It is more important to have people working together where collectively the network of individuals has the skills and the knowledge base. The music of a full orchestra produces a different experience of sound than does each individual instrument. So, too, will the experience and innovation of a network of skilled people create more robust outcomes and impact.

12
ABCD: Asset-Based Community Development

ABCD is primarily relationship building for action for a collective purpose, a path to organize groups and people in a community to act together for the common good. The focus is upon building power (the ability to act effectively) through relationships.

—MIKE GREEN

A GUIDE TO:

- The ABCD framework
- Shifting from a deficit-based mindset to asset-based mindset
- Putting people at the center of change
- Fostering ownership to build momentum for change

ASSET-BASED COMMUNITY DEVELOPMENT is rooted in the central idea that communities can act on their own to solve their most pressing challenges. Communities embrace the idea that the change they seek is best tackled by residents acting together as opposed to waiting for some outside force to change their circumstances. By moving from the mindset of change being "done *to*" to change being "done *with*," we fundamentally rethink our approach. ABCD starts with the premise that residents have gifts that they want to share and that harnessing these assets creates a powerful force for change, as opposed to the notion that a community is made up of the various deficits and challenges that need to be overcome. ABCD skills include uniting people as a whole community, building relationships, and fostering ownership to build momentum for change. By involving everyone in the process of change, we create more equitable communities.

I have increasingly used the ABCD skill set developed by John McKnight and Jodi Cressman in my work of community change. ABCD's approach taps into the single greatest untapped resource of community—its people. ABCD is a methodology that looks at the gifts and assets of people within a neighborhood or community that allow them to respond to and create local opportunities. ABCD's emphasis is on strengths, connections, citizen leadership, and the recognition that individual gifts become powerful when they are connected.

Key Contributions to Community Change

ABCD is about a mindset shift from "I am the expert and am here to help" to "I am here to listen to you and help you realize your dreams." This mental shift can be challenging for those who work in the helping professions and are trained to solve problems quickly. ABCD provides the best framework I know for building the kind of community change that will lead to breakthrough and population-level outcomes.

These are the seven core ideas of ABCD as articulated by John McKnight and adapted here:

1. EVERYONE HAS GIFTS

Each person in a community has something to contribute!

2. RELATIONSHIPS BUILD COMMUNITY

People must be connected for sustainable development.

3. CITIZENS AT THE CENTER

Citizens must be viewed as actors—not as passive recipients.

4. LEADERS INVOLVE OTHERS

Strength comes from a broad base of community action.

5. PEOPLE CARE

Listening to people's interests challenges myths of apathy.

6. LISTEN

Decisions should come from conversations where people are truly heard.

7. ASK

Generating ideas by asking questions is more sustainable than giving solutions.

ABCD asks us to consider these seven core ideas and actions that drive the work of breakthrough community change. They are foundational to all community change and provide a simple guide to ensure we recognize that everyone cares and that they have ideas and gifts to contribute to the change we seek.

When applied to breakthrough community change, ABCD acknowledges that communities are filled with assets and recognizes that members have strengths and talents to contribute. A strengths-based approach harnesses the assets by involving people and then collaboratively moving toward the kind of community they want. A deficit-based approach starts by identifying what is wrong in a community and asks how to fix it.

ABCD helps communities build their vision of their hoped-for future. ABCD includes strategies to help the community identify and build on the gifts people have and want to contribute. A key mantra in the ABCD community is "By us—For us." The desire of professionals is often to change communities with their ideas and expertise. They might say, "We know better than the residents." ABCD reminds us to listen to the community, understand their needs and ideas, and work with them to realize their vision.

ABCD fosters a sense of optimism, a desire to involve everyone, and the belief that together we are enough. We start from the place of believing that we have everything we need in our community to create a place that is good for all. If we work together, we can achieve our hoped-for breakthrough. This core premise combined with ideas of community engagement and collective impact can create a powerful force for change.

ABCD is foundational for equitable outcomes in all community change efforts. To believe that solutions can be imposed upon people; that those who are strong can speak for those who are not; and that power is about positions, education, and status is to build a society of haves and have-nots. Community change requires everyone to be involved, active, and engaged. A common agenda changes everything only if it is equitable and includes everyone.

Applying the Approach

In addition to the seven core ideas described above, ABCD researchers have identified eight core principles that, when applied as skill sets, make the work of community change practical. In my experience, these principles permeate much of the work that leads to breakthroughs in community change.

By utilizing **the positive principle** and focusing on what is strong, not what is wrong, I have been able to overcome my instinct to fix problems by offering my solutions and expertise. It has helped me to enter the work of community change by believing that communities have more assets than deficits. When I focus on the assets, the problems in a community seem smaller. When I work to end poverty within a community of one hundred thousand people that has 20 percent of the population living in poverty, it is easy to feel overwhelmed and think we need to move twenty thousand people toward a better future. But when you consider that 80 percent of the population does not live in poverty, you begin to see all the community systems that are working well. You also realize that you have one hundred thousand people to help you.

Using **the ownership principle**, I am reminded that a community has the power to set the vision for its projects. When they use their resources and do the work themselves, they have a far greater chance of success. Large-scale change requires us to involve everyone if we are to sustain the outcomes we hope to achieve. Every solution requires people to be committed to the desired outcome and feel a personal connection to making it work. Bringing clean water to a community requires more than just providing the technology for clean water. Clean water requires an entire infrastructure and modified behaviors (like using toilets or building safe septic systems) if we are to sustain the outcomes. A community that has created a common vision and mutual commitment to the outcome will sustain it.

Using **the wholeness principle** ensures everyone is included in the community-building process, including the weak, the poor, and the voiceless. Full inclusion increases cooperation, sharing, and trust, which will ultimately lead to a healthier, more resilient community. Equitable and racism-free communities do not happen because we wish them to be so. We need new ideas for development. At its core, ABCD embraces the idea of inclusion and wholeness. ABCD, first and foremost, values those outcomes that are generated by everyone for the good of everyone.

I love using **the wonderful principle**. When people are given the space and freedom to ask questions and imagine possibilities, the community is better able to discover what it truly cares about and desires to achieve. Breakthrough community change requires people to dream about a better future. Without dreams, hope dies. There is plenty of time for practical strategies in the planning process. But first, we must overcome feelings of hopelessness and cultivate a firm belief that a better future is possible.

The organic principle advances the idea that both the power and the blueprint for community growth lie within the community itself. We often talk about "bottom-up" community development. Community-based solutions as a way of thinking and approaching whole community change are integral for ABCD. Engaging the community and a common commitment is always the starting point for whole community change.

The momentum principle reminds us that success is in the very act of moving toward the goals that the community begins to uncover. Breakthrough community change starts slow and then grows, often rapidly. This is because momentum builds around the cheer "We did it!" This cheer symbolizes a sense of accomplishment, fosters a common commitment, and strengthens the belief that more can be done. This cheer begs the question, How can I contribute? Population-level change is not possible without building community-wide momentum.

The relational principle reminds us that strong and dynamic linkages between people in the community, both formal and informal, are the building blocks necessary for positive community change. To change a whole community is to build the communication channels "in between" people to strengthen trust. My colleague Liz Weaver is fond of saying, "We grow at the speed of trust." Relationships, empathetic communication, and active respect for others' ideas are at the core of whole community change.

The transformation principle gives me the greatest hope for a more equitable world. The key ingredient to creating positive community change is people who have moved from a self-perception of weakness and dependency to a new paradigm of dignity and self-respect. Dignity and self-respect are the foundation for believing in a better and more equitable future. From here people can more fully utilize the tools and resources available to them for personal change.

The value of applying ABCD skills, knowledge, and ideas to the work of breakthrough community change is that it provides a critical framework for the change ahead of us. By recognizing gifts and building relationships, we put people at the center of the change. Leaders utilizing ABCD thinking involve all the people who care in a community, rather than just professionals. ABCD encourages people to listen to each other and ask questions to evoke gifts and dreams rather than offering solutions. The ABCD approach provides a methodology for inclusion and mutuality that leads to more equitable and fair communities that are free of racism.

For Further Learning

Diers, Jim. *Neighbor Power: Building Community the Seattle Way.* Seattle: University of Washington Press, 2014.

McKnight, John, and Peter Block. *The Abundant Community: Awakening the Power of Families and Neighborhoods.* Oakland, CA: Berrett-Koehler Publishers, 2012.

McKnight, John L., and John P. Kretzmann. *Building Communities from the Inside Out: A Path Toward Finding and Mobilizing a Community's Assets.* Evanston, IL: Center for Urban Affairs and Policy Research Northwestern University, 1993.

Russell, Cormac. *Rekindling Democracy: A Professional's Guide to Working in Citizen Space.* Eugene, OR: Cascade Books, 2020.

Russell, Cormac, and John McKnight. *The Connected Community: Discovering the Health, Wealth, and Power of Neighborhoods.* Oakland, CA: Berrett-Koehler Publishers, 2022.

Also, the Asset-Based Community Development Institute has an exceptional website that posts continuous learning and best practices: *ABCDinstitute.org.*

13
Collective Impact

Shifting from isolated impact to collective impact is not merely a matter of encouraging more collaboration or public-private partnerships. It requires a systemic approach to social impact that focuses on the relationships between organizations and the progress toward shared objectives.

—JOHN KANIA AND MARK KRAMER

A GUIDE TO:

- Understanding the collective impact framework
- Establishing a system for continuous communication
- Fostering relationships between organizations
- Centering equity in the process of change
- Developing a mindset for a movement-building paradigm

COLLECTIVE IMPACT (CI) IS a powerful set of ideas and strategies. A community united in a common agenda and acting together for breakthrough change requires good tools and processes to take the work to scale. CI is the most advanced form of collaborative action currently available. The skills include building a common agenda and a shared measurement system, which make it easier for a community and its partners to work together, create opportunities, and strengthen mutually reinforcing activities. The skill of continuous communication keeps the partners aligned and builds momentum, while the backbone governance and staffing model provides an agreed-upon structure for action and dedicated professionals to support its implementation.

CI theory and practice provide some of the most important skill sets for breakthrough community change thinking and action. CI provides an opportunity for whole system integration and proven social technology that drives outcomes and impact. To realize a breakthrough, all community change requires us to understand the CI approach. I have yet to find a better social technology for large-scale change and sustained population-level outcomes. As a disciplined form of multisector collaboration, CI advances breakthrough community change by inviting changemakers to co-create a shared incubator space that focuses on advancing transformational outcomes and impact.

Key Contributions to Community Change

In 2011 John Kania and Mark Kramer's article "Collective Impact" was published in the winter issue of the *Stanford Social Innovation Review* and has since become one of the most downloaded articles in the magazine's history.[1] The approach described as CI was endorsed by the White House Council on Community Solutions under President Barack Obama and is now widely used to significantly improve outcomes on an array of complex social and environmental issues. As CI practitioners apply the CI framework, important insights and lessons are generated and generously shared. CI research lays the foundation for what is now a robust global field of practice.

Breakthrough community change requires a highly refined understanding of collaboration. CI promotes cooperation that points all efforts toward an impact. CI is about building unity by inviting individuals and organizations to orchestrate together through the development of a common agenda and shared measurement system. CI is working together across sectors to develop mutually reinforcing activities while building momentum through continuous communication. CI advances a backbone structure that acts like a conductor supported by a staff team to give leadership to the collaborative process.

The CI framework includes the following five conditions for impact:

- A common agenda
- A shared measurement agreement
- Multisector or mutually reinforcing activities
- Continuous communication and community engagement
- A strong backbone infrastructure

When all five conditions are brought together, a community-led leadership team supports the creation of a shared vision, plan, and common commitment to change by coordinating the efforts of diverse partners. The CI framework moves beyond simply collaborating. CI practitioners seek to co-create a coordinated strategy and shared commitment to addressing a complex issue.

There is a growing body of evidence that CI thinking and action can create population-level outcome change. The evaluation *When Collective Impact Has an Impact,* conducted collaboratively by ORS Impact and Spark Policy Institute, found that twenty of the twenty-five CI initiatives studied demonstrated population-level changes, which the evaluators defined as "changes for specific people within specific systems, geographic areas, or with specific needs."[2] Furthermore, these population-level changes "generally stemmed from changes in services, practices, and policies." Seven of the eight in-depth site visits revealed "strong or compelling data linking new or expanded programs/services or practice improvements in the CI initiatives to the population change."[3] Three sites demonstrated "strong evidence linking the different components of the initiatives' work to the change, and no plausible alternative hypotheses to better explain or augment our understanding of how change happened."

Applying the Approach

Shifting from isolated impact, where one agency is addressing a social issue, to a collective impact, where a community change is addressed by multiple partners, is not merely a matter of encouraging more collaboration or public-private partnerships. It requires the skills to develop a systemic approach to social impact. Skilled CI practitioners foster relationships between organizations to enable progress toward shared objectives. The key outcome of a collective impact approach is to support diverse actors in a community to work through a common agenda for change.

CI asks us to first take stock of the following *preconditions of success.* These preconditions would be the same for any form of large-scale effort for community change.

- The community has a demonstrated **history of collaboration** in addressing social issues and, more specifically, the issue the group is focusing on. A strong history of collaboration ensures the fundamentals of collaboration are widely understood.

- **System leaders are supportive** of the change being considered. These include leading community-based organizations, key government officials, business and community leaders, activists, and those with lived/living experience. Support from strong system leaders means that systemic change on the issue is desired.

- **Funder commitment** is critical, not only because the large-scale change requires funding but also because funders can be key blockers to system change. It is difficult for a community to mobilize toward change if funders continue to invest only in the status quo.

- There must be **community will** for the desired change. The issue you are addressing must be important to the community and often reported about in the media or highlighted in key reports.

CI practitioners seek to implement five key skill sets for a collective impact to be successful:

- They work toward a **common agenda** and a collective commitment to the desired outcome. A common agenda ensures that there is a whole community response and collaborative action where multiple organizations are implementing a joint community plan.

- They use a **shared measurement system** to determine a common understanding of the issue being addressed and, more importantly, a common measure of the desired outcome.

- Collaborating through **mutually reinforcing activities** ensures that the desired outcome is addressed by community-based organizations, government, businesses, and people with lived/living experience of the issue. Multisector action teams are often formed to implement key strategic directions identified in the community plan.

- Through **continuous communication** CI practitioners ensure that the many actors remain focused, and that the broader community is committed to change. A strong flow of information, continuous consultation, and promoting opportunities for involvement ensure that community partners are engaged.

- The skill sets required to form and support the **backbone role or infrastructure** are critical to the success of CI. This is more than a governance model. It is a recognition that large-scale collaborations require deliberate support and a system of organizing that keeps the actors working together and focused on real outcomes.

CI thinking is evolving. The publication of the seminal paper *Collective Impact 3.0* by Tamarack's Liz Weaver and Mark Cabaj marked another milestone in the understanding and evolving practice of CI.[4] They argued for an upgrade of the original CI framework based on two primary reasons. First, there had been enough experimentation with CI in a variety of contexts to appreciate and understand some of its limitations. Second, there was an opportunity to strengthen the skill sets of CI by weaving it together with the rich tradition of other well-established approaches to community change. The process described in Part I of this book is an example of how CI can be integrated with other effective skill sets and practices for whole community change.

Collective Impact 3.0 calls for incorporating a new leadership paradigm that extends the "shared management" mindset outlined in the initial CI research to also incorporate a "movement-building" paradigm. This new skill set heightens the importance of a diverse network of relationships and the need to engage others in exploring, contributing, and co-creating solutions to address it. When the shared management skill set's emphasis on generating results is combined with the movement-building skill set's focus on opening up "people's hearts and minds to new possibilities, we create the receptive climate for new ideas to take hold and embolden policymakers and system leaders."[5]

In February 2022 leaders in CI work wrote an article that was published in the *Stanford Social Innovation Review*. This article, "Centering Equity in Collective Impact," marked the beginning of a new chapter in CI research and practice. The authors sought to redefine CI efforts to include centering equity as a prerequisite. They have proposed a redefinition of the concept of collective impact as "a network of community members, organizations, and institutions that advance equity by learning together, aligning, and integrating their actions to achieve population- and systems-level change." The authors argued that centering equity alters the way practitioners implement collective impact. They provided five strategies they found critical for centering equity. These are early days for this new development, but this research has already made a significant contribution to the understanding of and focus on CI for future development.

An important criticism of CI is that the body of practice does not adequately recognize that it requires a highly advanced understanding of the work of community development and collaboration. I find it important to consider CI as a description of activities and skill sets that can be implemented in a variety of ways to improve outcomes. I do not believe that it is useful to understand CI as a prescribed set of ideas that need to be followed precisely. I prefer to use collective impact in an active sense rather than as a fixed descriptor: "We are striving for a collective impact by working together" rather than "We are a collective impact project."

For Further Learning

Kania, John, and Mark Kramer. "Collective Impact." *Stanford Social Innovation Review* 9, no. 1 (Winter 2011): 36–41.

Kania, John, Junious Williams, Paul Schmitz, Sheri Brady, Mark Kramer, and Jennifer Splansky Juster. "Centering Equity in Collective Impact." *Stanford Social Innovation Review* 20, no. 1 (2021): 38–45. *https://doi.org/10.48558/RN5M-CA77.*

ORS Impact and Spark Policy Institute. *When Collective Impact Has an Impact: A Cross-Site Study of 25 Collective Impact Initiatives.* Seattle and Denver: ORS Impact and Spark Policy Institute, 2018.

Weaver, Liz, ed. *The Journey of Collective Impact: Contributions to the Field from Tamarack Institute.* Victoria, BC: Friesen Press, 2019.

Weaver, Liz, and Mark Cabaj. *Collective Impact 3.0: An Evolving Framework for Community Change.* Waterloo, ON: Tamarack Institute, 2016.

Also, the Collective Impact Forum has an exceptional website that posts continuous learning and best practices: *CollectiveImpactForum.org.*

14

Community Engagement

When engagement is done well, we see outcomes like whole communities rallying together around a shared issue. We see people with lived experience who have previously been excluded being given leadership roles and the power to effect change. We see less polarization and more unification despite diverse perspectives. We see people who were previously protective of their resources now sharing and understanding that everyone is better off if they work together.

—LISA ATTYGALLE

A GUIDE TO:

- A framework for community engagement
- Reaching the hard to reach
- Shifting mindsets
- Creating resonance with allied groups

COMMUNITY ENGAGEMENT KNOWLEDGE and skills are extremely important because sustainable community change requires everyone in a community to be engaged, not just the traditional leaders and organizations associated with the issue. Engaging people is an essential skill for large-scale change to occur. We need to utilize listening, outreach, and organizational skills to engage many people who believe in the cause and are willing to act. I have observed that people become committed and actively participate in the work of large-scale community change when they have good information, are consulted about the desired change, and have opportunities to be involved in the change process.

Community change to achieve breakthrough population-level outcomes requires citizens to be engaged by working and learning together on behalf of their communities to create and realize a bold common agenda. Community engagement is rooted in the belief that the best solutions to complex community issues are discovered when a dedicated group of community leaders from multiple perspectives build trust and work together to better align their efforts.

It is important to consider that authentic, equitable community engagement takes more time and resources than what most communities are used to. Taking equity into consideration while embarking on community engagement is paramount. Reaching the hard to reach involves developing a strategy to do so, including identifying potential barriers to engagement, and identifying/building relationships with people who have prior relationships or connections to specific populations that you are seeking to engage.

Key Contributions to Community Change

For communities to be resilient and thrive, they need to be built on a foundation of care and deep connection. For communities to address complex issues, they need the skill sets to bring together many sectors and tap into the potential of citizen leadership. Communities become more resilient when they strengthen their natural networks of care. Community engagement skills play a foundational role in helping to nurture and create an enabling environment to foster the necessary community leadership for community change efforts to thrive.

The skill sets of authentic community engagement require leaders to have an attitude of curiosity, focus on aspirations, and enjoy continuous learning. The power of a strongly held and shared community aspiration anchors people to their community and a common purpose. This is an important step in moving a common agenda forward and identifying manageable pockets of change that help the community to achieve the quick wins that generate trust, stronger relationships, and greater confidence in the capability of their community.

By engaging people with lived experience of the issue we are addressing, we provide a forum to discuss how the work of community change will advance equity in the community. By working across key sectors, we can unify a community and ensure that all voices are heard.

Applying the Approach

Community Engagement and Movement Building

Liz Weaver of the Tamarack Institute shares, "A modern paradox faced by community changemakers is that, while today's networked world makes it easier than ever to mobilize support around ideas, the complexity of the issues facing our communities, combined with a scarcity of funding and shrinking public attention spans, has made the work of mobilizing for lasting systems change more difficult than ever."[1]

Bringing a lens of movement building to the work of community engagement has proven to be an important evolution. Jason Mogus, principal strategist with NetChange, proposes The Directed-Network Campaign Approach and highlights four useful principles to consider.[2]

- Give members an active role in shaping their own direction and greater ability to customize their participation. This approach increases enthusiasm for and commitment to the campaign and often benefits from key insights and member-generated innovations.

- Rather than trying to "own" an issue, focus attention on creating resonance with allied groups and providing ways for them to collectively focus their power simultaneously.

- Key ingredients in building a compelling cause include great storytelling; a simple and believable rationale for why audiences should care about the issue; the illustration of a path to victory; and the identification of clear roles for members.

- Be disciplined in tracking progress, and prototype key messages and deployment strategies. Utilize the network's power only when clear winnable moments are identified. This conserves resources for the long-term work required to achieve systems change.

Authentic community engagement requires skills, a long-term commitment to relationship building, and an investment of adequate resources so that engagement becomes more than a one-off event that occurs only at the start of an initiative. To fully harness the extraordinary power of ordinary people, community engagement should be a pillar within every effective community change strategy.

A Mindset Shift Is Required

A significant challenge to the practice of community engagement is the growing levels of loneliness and the lack of a sense of belonging in all age groups. The experience of social isolation has a significant negative impact on how connected and committed people feel to their communities and to each other. The individual's sense of belonging is directly relevant to those of us concerned with the engagement of our community. Researchers have found that there is a direct correlation between people feeling a sense of belonging and their subsequent willingness to act for the common good.

A mindset shift is required for individuals to move beyond seeing themselves solely as recipients of service or sources of information to seeing their responsibility to be participants and leaders in generating the kind of communities they want to be part of. For organizations, the mindset shift is one from seeing themselves primarily as "the doers" and providers of programs and services to embracing a role as the catalysts for change. As organizations begin to see themselves as co-facilitators of conversations and multisector collaborations that share a commitment, the well-being of a community is strengthened.

Inform–Consult–Involve

I would suggest that people become engaged in a breakthrough community change initiative when they receive good information about the problem they care about and understand that working together to achieve a collective impact is a process needed to address it. People also become engaged when they are consulted to provide their ideas and respond to the ideas of their peers. When people see ways of giving their talents and contributing their assets to build a better future, they increase their commitment to the work.

The "three sisters" of **inform, consult, and involve** work best when applied continuously. A constant cycle of informing, consulting, and involving people results in deeper personal and organizational engagement. Collective engagement happens when people connect together to learn, discuss, and work on common issues.

Community Conversations

Community conversation skill sets are critical to collective engagement. These conversations build a collective commitment to action. When we bring people together in conversation to discuss good information, they engage in a form of collective learning. Community conversations create a container for people to hear each other's opinions and to find agreement across opinions.

As I share in my book *Community Conversations*, creating a space in which those involved can get to know, understand, and trust one another is critical to community change. Trust is important because it allows people to open up to new ideas and suspend what they know to be true. They also create a space to learn together. In some ways, the space we create together is like a ship for exploring new seas. A key outcome of the conversation is the ability of a diverse group of people to come to a common understanding.

The role of these conversations is to bring together the people in a community who can contribute to the success of the initiative being promoted. By working together, people can change the way a community addresses a particular issue and improve the quality of life on many levels. Like a tide that lifts all boats, community conversations enable real and lasting community change.

Equity: Engaging Lived and Living Experience

The skill to meaningfully engage residents and people with lived experiences as leaders and co-designers of new solutions is at the heart of the practice of community engagement. These individuals are often referred to as *context experts*. They bring a deep appreciation of the unique characteristics of the place where the innovation is to be implemented. This knowledge is invaluable as you develop strategies that will capitalize on the strengths and mitigate the limitations of your community.

Context experts are people with lived/living experiences who deeply understand the realities of their needs. People with lived/living experiences are those individuals that will benefit the most, should we be successful. If we are reducing poverty, it is those who have or are experiencing poverty that will benefit the most. If we are tackling climate change, it would be young people. If we are tackling more age-friendly communities, it would be seniors.

Recognizing people with lived/living experiences as context experts is an integral mindset to developing the skills needed for authentic community engagement. People with lived/living experience work alongside content experts in the government, business, and nonprofit sectors to challenge power imbalances. The voices of all context experts are critical to balance and counter the tendency for *content* experts to dominate agendas, discussions, and, ultimately, decisions. The invaluable expertise of these context experts with lived/living experiences adds strength and resiliency to poverty-reduction work. Their first-hand knowledge of systemic barriers is invaluable in co-creating innovative solutions to overcome them.

Alison Homer, through the Tamarack Institute, worked with a team of people with lived/living experiences for many months to determine key principles and skill sets that can be considered best practices and add important insight into the work of engaging people with lived/living experiences when considering a breakthrough community change approach:[3]

- Commit to creating safer spaces that support open dialogue across diverse perspectives. Groups that effectively engage people with lived/living experiences build mutual respect and establish a level of trust that supports open dialogue across a diversity of perspectives. They ensure that everyone at the table feels comfortable and included, and they identify ways that each person can apply their unique talents and expertise to move the work forward.

- Groups that effectively engage people with lived/living experiences embrace diversity, equity, and inclusion as core values in their work. Borrowed from disability justice movements, "nothing about us without us" is an ideology that is often adopted by poverty reduction groups when engaging people with lived/living experiences.

- Develop meetings and agendas with people in mind. Inclusive structures, policies, and practices help create safer spaces that promote the full participation of people with lived/living experiences. These include group norms, committee structures, roundtable agreements, meeting practices, and written policies such as diversity and social inclusion plans.

- Reframe the dominant narrative wisdom that people with lived/living experiences bring to the table, but also create opportunities for these individuals to share their perspectives and, importantly, to influence decisions. Groups can work toward including people with lived/ living experience across all organizational structures, such as boards, tables, committees, subcommittees, and action teams. They can also create opportunities for participation across meetings, consultations, and other engagements.

- Ensure that no one incurs a cost to engage. Ensuring that everybody at the table is fairly supported plays a major role in breaking down barriers to participation and in leveling the playing field between those who are and those who are not paid to engage in the work. Poverty reduction groups should therefore first and foremost ensure that people with lived/living experience do not incur participation-related expenses. At a minimum, this requires groups to provide for or reimburse partners with lived/living experiences for food and transportation. Additional services, such as childcare, interpretation, and notetaking, may also be required. For workshops and conferences, it is helpful if groups can cover costs of flights and accommodation, waive registration fees or offer scholarships, and pay per diems.

- Different people require different supports to participate. Some people attend meetings and events as part of paid employment, while others contribute voluntarily. While salaried individuals (such as government and nonprofit staff) are more likely to be paid, particularly when engagements take place during regular business hours, people with lived/living experience of poverty often donate their time. These individuals can face associated barriers to participation, such as living on modest fixed incomes, working for low wages, or juggling more than one job. They are more likely to experience financial difficulties to participate in the process. For example, attending an engagement event might require them to miss work and forgo the money from that day's wages.

- Advocacy is only heard once trust is built. Maintaining a foundation of trust is fundamental to the meaningful engagement of people with lived/living experience. In contrast, a lack of trust serves as a huge barrier to participation. People with lived/living experiences may have had negative, trauma-based experiences in past interactions when working within human services systems. Trust within a multiprofit poverty reduction initiative can therefore take a long time to build, particularly in instances where a person has been let down in the past, and where they feel like trust needs to be rebuilt.

- Authentic engagement is about sharing power. No matter how well intentioned the group, power relationships creep into social spaces. Conventional decision-making processes can perpetuate power imbalances and disenfranchise those who already feel unheard. Voices are often accorded different levels of influence and speaking time based on status quo demographics, such as sector represented or professional status.

- Drive engagement by mentorship and process. Support engagement by investing in capacity building and skill development. Engagement promotes teamwork and builds trust. Community groups need to work more inclusively with colleagues with lived/living experiences. Training builds confidence, deepens participation, and can support groups to move from service providers to collaborators to allies of people with lived/living experience.

• Foster an inclusive space that reflects the diversity of the community to better understand people's experiences, overcome tokenism, and balance group dynamics. Groups should aim to reflect the true diversity of their communities within the spaces of their own work.

Developing the skill set for engaging and involving people with lived and living experiences is critical to breakthrough community change. By ensuring the whole community is engaged, we can get as close as possible to the problem we are addressing. This can result in better, more equitable outcomes.

Engaged citizens are a tremendous source of ingenuity and creativity. They are the greatest untapped resource for solving the most complex and intractable issues of our time. The knowledge, passion, and capabilities of community residents are frequently underutilized. Community members are sources of innovation and much-needed resources in the implementation of promising solutions to our toughest social and environmental issues.

For Further Learning

Attygalle, Lisa. *Creating a Culture for Community Engagement: How Fear May Be Holding Us Back from Authentic Engagement*. Waterloo, Ontario: Tamarack Institute, 2020.

Attygalle, Lisa. *Understanding Community-Led Approaches to Community Change.* Waterloo, Ontario: Tamarack Institute, 2020.

Born, Paul. *Community Conversations: Mobilizing the Ideas, Skills, and Passion of Community Organizations, Governments, Businesses, and People.* Toronto: BPS Books, 2012.

Born, Paul. *Deepening Communities: Finding Joy Together in Chaotic Times.* San Francisco: Berrett-Koehler Publishers, 2014.

Homer, Alison. *Engaging People with Lived/Living Experience: A Guide for Including People in Poverty Reduction.* Waterloo, Ontario: Tamarack Institute, 2020.

Also, the Tamarack Institute has an exceptional website that posts continuous learning and best practices: *Tamarack Community.ca.*

15

Community Innovation

Social innovation is an initiative, product, process, or program that profoundly changes the basic routines, resource and authority flows, or beliefs of any social system. Successful social innovations have durability and broad impact.

—FRANCES WESTLEY

A GUIDE TO:

- A framework for community innovation
- Shifting from the mindset of being powerless recipients to creative shapers of change
- Thinking beyond the usual way of doing things

COMMUNITY INNOVATION IS A CENTRAL concept of the breakthrough community change approach. To innovate, we must do more than work harder, smarter, or invest more money in the current way of doing things. Change at the community level requires skills and knowledge that help us to rethink current systems of program delivery. It requires us to come up with new ideas. It requires us to be creative and think beyond the usual ways of doing things. It requires us to understand design thinking. It requires us to reach out across sectors. It requires us to reach out to people most affected by the issue we are trying to address.

Innovation can be described as the intentional cultivation of new ways of thinking and learning. The way that we think influences the options we can see and determines the choices we can make. To achieve a breakthrough in community change requires us to have the skill sets to innovate together. These include the ability to think and learn together, develop a common agenda for change, and work together differently. Innovation is also the introduction of something new and useful, such as prototypes, new models, and/or novel solutions that positively impact the community's core issue. This is community innovation.

Key Contributions to Community Change

Community innovation is a form of social innovation in that the innovation is place-based within the specific geography of a community. As dynamic living labs, communities offer the perfect container for innovation. We have come to understand that to be effective, innovation requires both an appreciation of the issue being addressed as well as a deep understanding of the unique characteristics of the community.

We need to understand the place and the people within the community where the innovation will be implemented. Innovations that have proven successful in one community can, at best, serve as a source of inspiration for another. Innovations translated into place must be adapted and modified to the unique circumstances and assets available if they are to maximize the strengths and assets of the community where they hope to be replicated.

Community innovation is not just a lofty theoretical pursuit reserved solely for experts and academics. In his book *Impact: Six Patterns to Spread Your Social Innovation*, Al Etmanski reminds us that "humans' ingenuity and creativity in the face of adversity is what defines us as a species."[1] In every community, ordinary citizens—individuals, neighbors, and families—are constantly hard at work striving to make things better. Etmanski refers to these individuals as passionate amateurs who "are motivated by necessity and inspired by love. Someone or something they care about is vulnerable, under siege, or in trouble and they have no choice but to respond."

Rarely are "passionate amateurs" successful in advancing community innovation alone. It is when these individuals join together in a movement and team up with champions from diverse sectors that promising ideas evolve and have a lasting impact that changes systems. The complex nature of our communities' most intractable issues requires wisdom and insights from multiple sectors working together to generate measurable and lasting change.

Applying the Approach

As living systems, communities are continually evolving and changing. The promise of community innovation is the belief that we do not need to remain powerless recipients of the whims of change, but rather that, together and with proper skill sets, we are capable of shaping and guiding the changes unfolding around us in ways that help to orchestrate a better future for all.

The goal of community innovation is to create sufficient local interest and capacity to undertake a whole community change initiative. Innovation can be both creative and entre-preneurial. The creative skill set is about engaging as many people as possible to build deeper insight into the dynamics of the issue. The goal is to develop as many solutions, even out-of-the-box solutions, as possible. The entrepreneurial skill set is about identifying the opportunities most likely to move the entire group forward and for which the community will invest energy, time, and money.

Moving from Exploration to Development

Consider that community innovation cycles through various phases of development.

In the exploration phase, we test ideas, learn together, and begin to come up with various strategies for change. People in the exploration phase deepen their engagement and are encouraged to think creatively. The required skill sets are described in Chapter 4, which discusses how people with a shared vision or commitment begin to explore new and inno-vative ideas. As they test these ideas in the community, they are looking to expand possibilities and see which ideas reso-nate with most people with a goal of community acceptance.

As we move into the developmental phase, people need to agree on the strategy they will deploy and choose the ideas for change that will have the greatest impact. The skills to sup-port this stage are described in Chapters 4 and 5 and include the process of writing a community plan and helping groups pick which strategies will have the greatest impact and which ideas have the strongest buy-in—an important skill set. Other important skill sets include writing the strategy, testing the idea with stakeholders, and finally supporting others so that ideas are further developed and refined.

As we move into the production phase, the community leadership seeks to achieve scale, including a system- or population-level change. The skill sets required at this phase are described in the implementation sections of Part I of this book and in Chapter 7.

As we move into the creative destruction phase, a community needs to consider if they will renew their strategy or close it. The skill sets to support this stage are described in Chapter 9 and include strong consultation and engagement skills.

Each stage of the development cycle requires innovative skill sets.[2]

Through each of the stages, we seek community innovation by:

- Seeking to deepen engagement so more people are involved and commitment grows
- Growing momentum to build credibility and capacity
- Using emergence thinking to guide us (the group learns together and adapts and refines ideas)
- Networking so that the community plan is community owned and resourced
- Creating an innovative organizing structure that supports the desired change

Innovation as community change can best be understood as a process implemented by a community of people in hopes of finding a better way forward together. Sometimes this new way forward is a social innovation, a new idea that creates a better result, but most often a community innovation supports new ways of thinking and of acting together as a community. Community innovation in this way is highly emergent. Ideas are developed, tested, implemented, and then continuously refined. Effective community innovation is about good ideas for sure, but it requires a community of people willing to change their collective approach, and therefore, the skill sets of implementing a community innovation are innovative.

For Further Learning

Etmanski, Al. *Impact: Six Patterns to Spread Your Social Innovation.* Vancouver, BC: Orwell Cove, 2015.

Isaacs, William. *Dialogue and the Art of Thinking Together.* New York: Doubleday, 1999.

Stewart, Chené. *Re-authoring the World: The Narrative Lens and Practices for Organizations, Communities, and Individuals.* Johannesburg: KR Publishing, 2013.

Westley, Frances, and Nino Antadze. "Making a Difference: Strategies for Scaling Social Innovation for Greater Impact." *The Innovation Journal: The Public Sector Innovation Journal* 15, no. 2 (2010). *https://www.innovation.cc/scholarly-style/2010_15_2_2_westley-antadze_social-innovate.pdf.*

Westley, Frances, Brenda Zimmerman, and Michael Quinn Patton. *Getting to Maybe: How the World Is Changed.* Toronto: Random House Canada, 2006.

16
Collaborative Leadership

Collaborative leaders consistently demonstrate five qualities: the drive to achieve goals through collaboration; the ability to listen carefully to what is being said (and not said) to understand others' perspectives; the desire to look for win-win solutions; the use of pull techniques, rather than push, to accomplish goals; and the capacity to strategically connect projects to a larger purpose.

—DAVID CHRISLIP

A GUIDE TO:

- A framework for collaborative leadership
- Understanding that leadership is something we do together
- Developing key leadership attributes

COLLABORATIVE LEADERSHIP IS COMMUNITY change work on a personal level. It requires the people involved in the change process to consider how they show up in the work. I often express collaborative leadership in this way: I am a leader. We are all leaders. There is work to do. Let's get on with it. This provides a framework for building collective action. We can develop skills to recognize the leadership in an individual who desires change. When leaders become engaged, we deploy skills that help people take ownership of the change desired. Finally, we require skills to help leaders collectively engage and support them to join forces to create collaborative action.

The first time I met author Margaret Wheatley, she said something that stayed with me. She said (or at least this is how I heard it): "Do not worry about organizing people . . . when people are engaged, they will organize as they need to." Her book *Leadership and the New Science* inspired my thinking about systems change. In healthy community systems, leadership coexists when people are mutually reliant. Collaborative leadership leads to community change. Leadership is not purely an individual act. Leadership is something people do together. The idea that effective systems require many leaders to work together frightens and inspires me. As people work toward a common agenda, they bring a collective leadership to bear upon the issue they desire to address.

I have noticed such a dramatic difference in engagement and outcomes that result from leading with a positive spirit, a smile, words of encouragement, empathy, and compassion, and having universally accessible, open, transparent communication. Good leaders are not afraid of transparency. Fear of change sometimes evolves just from not knowing what is going on in your community or not understanding the process or the work and engagement that has already gone into something. Knowledge empowers. People feel respected and heard when others take the time to communicate something back to them. Good leaders might help people understand

and embrace their role in order not to be afraid to lead in that role as part of the collaborative.

Key Contributions to Community Change

When people are involved in making decisions and setting directions together, they take ownership, are more effective, and restore pride in their community. Community leaders create the conditions for people to participate and be reflective with each other. A community's commitment and performance increase exponentially with the degree of power, control, and ownership members feel they have in their own perceptions of the work that needs to be done.

In successful community change, participants work together as peers, share a collective fate, and bring their competencies to the table. They create a sense of community that breaks down barriers to opportunity as they share common perspectives, interests, and experiences. Community leadership enables such action.

Applying the Approach

Collective leadership requires distinct skills that draw people into the collective. We can observe community leadership skill sets on four levels.

First, individual leaders support the collaboration through personal contributions, such as:

- Sharing a personal vision
- Listening
- Analyzing the facts

- Giving direction
- Being bold

Second, groups can be observed as people collaborating by:

- Conversing
- Deepening relationships
- Agreeing
- Collaborating
- Acting in unison

Third, individual leaders support groups collaborating by:

- Enabling (supporting change)·
- Enlisting (inviting people into the change)
- Entrusting (trusting that people want what is best for all)
- Engaging (deepening community will for change)
- Envisioning (supporting a vision for a better future)

Fourth, collaborative leadership work includes:

- Process facilitation (supporting groups of people to make decisions)
- Nurturing leaders and collective leadership (mentoring and encouraging leadership)
- Developing relationships and interrelationships (building trust)
- Effective listening and communication skills (communicating well)
- Group facilitation (bringing groups together and facilitating discussion)

Collaborative leaders understand how each of these skills contributes to community change.

I asked three leaders who have shaped my thinking about community leadership to share their understanding of the value of and approach to community leadership required to be effective in producing community change breakthroughs.[1]

Megan Courtney, Inspiring Communities New Zealand

Kāore te kumara e kōrero ana mo tōna ake reka.
(The kumara does not brag about its own sweetness.)

For Māori, the whakataukī (proverb) above and the humility it engenders underpin the leadership culture in Aotearoa (New Zealand). When we started talking openly and proactively about growing leaders and leadership, the typical response was "Who, me? I'm not a leader." This has taken some time to break through!

LEADING IN LIVING SYSTEMS

Knowing that leadership is a key ingredient in living systems, we start from the position of leadership as collective work and the domain of everyone. Leaderful organizations (where many leaders coexist) help frame and communicate the aspiration of "leaderful communities." These leaders also put an early stake in the ground by defining leadership as intentional action by any individual or group that seeks to sustain and/or change the way things are.

LEADERSHIP IS CONTEXTUAL

In the early phases of community change, having individual leaders out front is essential. Without them, it's often difficult to generate the momentum and resources required to get and sustain lift-off. Longer-term success, however, equally relies on leaders with the skills to nurture and empower ownership and actively involve others. They also need to skillfully hold and balance polarities that are always in movements—such as diversity and inclusion, process and action, awareness of self and others, and having time and not having time.

LEADERSHIP AS LEARNING AND CHANGE

Seeing leadership as learning, best supported by processes of collective inquiry, takes the pressure off leaders to have the right answer for every situation. Noticing and naming what we're seeing, and taking time to make meaning together, makes the cues for what's next for us and others more obvious. In the process of collaborative inquiry, we grow the confidence and competence of all involved to play a part in leading. Sometimes that means stepping forward, stepping back, or even stepping right out.

Liz Weaver, The Tamarack Institute, Waterloo, Canada

The face of communities is changing. Communities are trying to cope with complex and interconnected challenges, which are exacerbated by an increased rate and pace of change. Even though the challenges are more complex, the capacity of leaders to adapt and cope with changes is often limited by the systems in which they work.

These five principles or skill sets provide directions for leaders coping with rapid and persistent community change. The principles are especially relevant to changemakers coping with adaptive and changing community environments and working to resolve complex challenges.

PRINCIPLE 1: MAKE THE VOICE OF THE PEOPLE CENTRAL

Engaging community or citizens' voices, particularly those individuals impacted by the problem trying to be solved, is critical to the success of any community change effort. Citizens with lived or direct experience bring an important perspective to the issue, as they are navigating the challenge regularly. They will have insights into what is or is not working and where changes need to be made. However, engaging citizens often means paying attention to building relationships and trust. We often have a bias toward working with those we already feel comfortable with. Engaging with others takes time, patience, and a focus on building connections.

PRINCIPLE 2: WORK ACROSS BOUNDARIES

Similar to engaging the voice of the people in community change efforts, tackling complex community challenges requires us to work across boundaries. This means engaging individuals and sectors that can play a pivotal and influential role in the community change effort. This also enables changemakers to leverage new and different resources than the sector actors can bring to the table.

PRINCIPLE 3: CATALYZE CHANGE AND WORK ADAPTIVELY

Communities are not static. There is a rhythm and an ebb and flow to them. Even as a collaborative group begins an intervention, changes emerge. Adaptive leadership is about having a micro and macro or systems vision. It is about catalyzing the changes as they emerge but also creating enough space to leverage new opportunities as they emerge.

PRINCIPLE 4: ENGAGE IN SYSTEMIC THINKING AND ACTION

Being able to ascertain the health of the entire forest as well as individual trees is an analogy for engaging in systemic thinking and action. This principle requires adaptive leaders to view their change efforts from different lenses: seeing and navigating the whole system, engaging different parts and resources in the system, and considering their roles as changemakers within the system. Having these three lenses enables changemakers to leverage opportunities as they emerge.

PRINCIPLE 5: BE COURAGEOUS

Adaptive leadership requires us to step outside our comfort zone and be bold. It is risky, and at times we might not get it right. It takes courage, purpose, and a relentless passion to work toward something better.

David Chrislip, Coauthor, Collaborative Leadership

The changes unfold around us in ways that help to orchestrate a better future for all.

Collaborative leaders seeking breakthroughs are decidedly visionary, but this vision is focused on how people can work together constructively, rather than on a particular vision or solution.[2]

Collaborative leaders define their roles and practices differently than traditional leaders, who are often tactical and positional. Here are six key skill sets of collaborative leaders:

- They inspire commitment and action. Power and influence help, but they are not the distinguishing features of collaborative leaders. The distinguishing feature is that these leaders initiate a process that brings people together when nothing else is working. They are action-oriented, but the action involves convincing people that something can be done, not telling them what to do or doing the work for them.

- They lead as a peer problem solver. Collaborative leaders help groups create visions and solve problems. They do not solve the problems for the group or engage in command-and-control behavior.

- They build broad-based involvement. Collaborative leaders take responsibility for the diversity of the group and make a conscious and disciplined effort to identify and bring together all the relevant stakeholders.

- They sustain hope and participation. Collaborative leaders convince participants that each person is valued, help set incremental and achievable goals, and encourage celebrations along the way.

- They embrace servant leadership. Collaborative leaders are servants of the group, helping stakeholders do their work and looking out to make sure those others' needs are met and that they grow as persons.

- They understand leadership as a process. Motivation and inspiration happen through the belief in the credibility of the collaborative process and good working relationships with many people.

Most often, community leadership supports collaboration. Community change requires us to collaborate. The skill sets of collaboration are critical for community leadership. Collaboration can be between people or communities. Leaders who are most effective in addressing public issues are not necessarily the ones who know the most about those issues.

Rather, they are the leaders who have the skill sets and can get the right people together to create visions. These leaders intuitively grasp the need for community collaboration and know when the community is ready to take on this challenge.

For Further Learning

Born, Paul. *Leaderful Communities: A Study in Community Leadership*. Saarbrücken, Germany: Verlag, 2008.

Brooks, David. "Winning the War on Poverty: The Canadians Are Doing It; We're Not." *New York Times*, April 4, 2019. *https://www.nytimes.com/2019/04/04/opinion/canada-poverty-record.html*.

Chrislip, David, and Carl Larson. *Collaborative Leadership: How Citizens and Civic Leaders Can Make a Difference*. San Francisco: Jossey-Bass, 1994.

Schmitz, Paul. *Everyone Leads: Building Leadership from the Community Up*. San Francisco: Jossey-Bass, 2011.

Wheatley, Margaret J. *Leadership and the New Science: Discovering Order in a Chaotic World*. 3rd Edition. San Francisco: Berrett-Koehler Publishers, 2006.

17

Evaluations That Support Community Change

*Social innovators, evaluators, and community
changemakers are increasingly focused on changing
complex systems, but often struggle to describe either
the systems themselves or what they hope to achieve.*

—MARK CABAJ

A GUIDE TO:

- A framework for evaluations that support community change
- Understanding multiple forms of evaluation
- Tracking population-level change

AT TAMARACK, WE FREQUENTLY consider skill sets at three levels of outcomes when we track large-scale community change. First, we require skills to track how many individuals and families have experienced an improvement in their lives because of the programs that have been put into place. Second, we need skills to track a community's potential by understanding and documenting how its capacity for change is improving. This involves learning to track outcomes such as expanded cross-sector collaboration, strengthened engagement with people of lived experience, or a more exact and broadly held understanding of the issue. Third, we want to develop skills to track large-scale sustainable change at the policy and systems level. Systems-level changes in approach to the issue on an organizational level or a community-wide level are tracked, as they are evidence of large-scale or population-level community change.

Participatory and collaborative forms of evaluation are essential for understanding the impact of breakthrough community change, as they recognize that collective change cannot scale unless we understand collaborative outcomes and approaches. A shared measurement system requires us to understand not only what we want to change, but also how we might be able to measure the change as real and tangible at the population level. Most essential is that the people who are acting together for change must be engaged to learn together. Their participation in the evaluation is critical to collective learning.

More formal evaluation is often required by funders, professionals, and governments. Traditional forms of evaluation can be useful, but often they are inadequate for understanding the complex nature of community change. Many more participatory forms of evaluation have emerged to meet this need.

Key Contributions to Community Change

The formal evaluation field that grew up in the 1960s and 70s established a pattern of evaluation that focused first on using formative evaluation to build and improve models, then summative evaluation to help external bodies judge the worth and scalability of the models and/or hold innovators accountable for keeping close to their original plans and objectives. Since then, evaluation has been self-correcting to deal with all the limitations of these important yet narrow approaches and trying to keep up with community changemakers.

There is a large body of knowledge, practice, and skill sets that can support community change evaluation. Make sure that any evaluator you bring in is aware of these principles and forms of evaluation. Here are five approaches to the evaluation I have found particularly useful:

Utilization-focused evaluation (UFE) strives to ensure that the evaluation is designed to be useful to the primary users. Michael Quinn Patton's book *Utilization-Focused Evaluation* had a profound impact on me.[1] I started to see evaluation not as something I feared, but rather as something that would help our collaborative team learn and improve. Three ideas are extremely useful in community change evaluation:

- First, UFE can be about learning together so we can improve future outcomes. As a group trying to figure out new and innovative ways to understand change, this meant we sought new ways to constantly gain insights that would surface new solutions. An evaluation that emphasizes learning over judging supports the continuous evolution of strategies.

- Second, UFE can be cooperative and a co-learning opportunity. When our utilization-focused evaluator first addressed us, it was to seek our questions. The key concept was to ask everyone who cares about the outcome what they want to learn from the evaluation. Next, ask them what questions they wanted to be answered. These comments and questions then formed the basis for the evaluation. People found the evaluation useful because it was answering the questions they wanted answered. The evaluation was their collective inquiry.

- Third, the UFE can be about identifying those factors that create outcomes as opposed to simply judging the work that has been done. This meant that we had an outside look at the ideas we were trying to implement. The evaluation would provide skilled insight into how we might improve to get better outcomes. This was the very definition of useful for our community.

Developmental evaluation (DE) helps us move away from fixed, externally driven evaluation designs to evaluations that are designed to provide changemakers with real-time feedback that is useful for continual development and adaptation. Often the DE evaluator is a participant in the ongoing reflection and planning with the Leadership Team. Ongoing reports help the team set goals and reflect on their achievements. My experience is that a DE is a form of coaching that is extremely useful in gaining ongoing insight into the work of community change.

Participatory evaluation engages the diversity of the community to ensure relevance, ownership, and richness of the evaluation process and findings. Participatory evaluation can be helpful to community change organizations. In these types of evaluation, the roles between the evaluator, the evaluation, and the team are balanced. The evaluator and community partners share the responsibility for the work of the evaluation. The evaluation team may be made up of community stakeholders. Together with an evaluator they are leading and controlling a shared process for decision-making, planning, design, implementation, and reporting. Often the Leadership Team, staff, and community partners are actively engaging with the evaluator to implement the evaluation process by supporting and sharing evidence and reporting.

Collaborative evaluation may be more typical and closest to the more traditional role of evaluation that we are used to. The professional evaluator is given the lead role in conducting the evaluation. Key stakeholders will be asked to participate and provide implementation support, but the professional evaluator is directly accountable for successfully rolling things out. Final decisions about planning, design, implementation, and reporting are all left to the evaluator with the support and input of collaboration members, who can include a range of stakeholders, from program staff to the community intervention team and participants.

Empowerment evaluation is valued for its focus on strategic learning and building the capacity of community stakeholders as they do an evaluation together. Empowerment evaluation focuses on fostering sustainability.[2] Findings and processes are often meant to encourage and move communities or groups to self-determination. The role of the evaluator in this scenario is commonly observed as less directly involved in all facets of the evaluation cycle from planning to reporting. Working side by side with the program staff or community team, the evaluator is engaged for their strong skills in listening, hosting community conversations, and teaching community stakeholders that are giving direction to the evaluation process. The evaluator, in this case, can be seen as a supportive friend or evaluation supporter and is engaged to "facilitate the process and steps of an empowerment evaluation including raising many of the difficult questions, and as appropriate, [telling] the hard truths diplomatically." This is similar to the role of the facilitator in developmental evaluation.

You may want to draw from any of these five forms of evaluation. What is most important is that your evaluator has a solid understanding of evaluations that takes into consideration the ideas and wishes of your collaborative partners.

Applying the Approach

Evaluators tell us that "you measure what you treasure." By setting specific goals that are measurable and achievable, we can report on how well we have achieved those goals. We are also told "you can only measure that which you can control." And since we cannot control the work of other organizations and sectors in our community, we often do not track community outcomes. The challenge is that as each community organization more narrowly defines their work by the outcomes they can track and control, the evaluations narrow in scope. These types of evaluations lose sight of the fact that our combined efforts are what shape our community's quality of life. For breakthroughs to occur, we need to learn and work together as one community.

At a minimum, we require the skill sets to broaden the scope of our evaluations. If my job were to help the unemployed, I would be measuring the number of people we served, their barriers to employment, and the interventions we deployed to help them. I would want to know how successful those interventions were. In community change evaluation, I would also want to measure how our work was contributing to the end of unemployment in our community and what contribution community partners have made to this goal. If I were treating cancer, I would want to know how the work of our hospital was contributing to reducing cancer rates in our community. If I were an educator, I would be tracking our contribution to graduation rates and entrance rates to higher education programs or employment.

There are several key principles and skill sets that have helped me to stay focused and ensure that the evaluations remain community-focused.

Evaluations Should Be Useful

Evaluations are useful when they generate new insights or understanding about the issue groups are addressing, such as key insights from clients or partners. These insights help them get closer to the community issue they are seeking to change. Evaluations are also useful for uncovering process improvements that can help organizations better do the work of community change.

Useful evaluations can complement the development process and give insight that will support better outcomes. Useful types of evaluations are also participatory and collaborative and empower the community partners to work better together. A useful evaluation can help your group understand how to achieve the breakthrough you desire. In this way, evaluation supports the learning process and helps a group adapt and change on their journey to impact.

Evaluations Should Be Responsive to Community Partners

Three principles are central in the process of designing an evaluation plan that is responsive to your community change partners.

First, community partners and people with lived experience should be included in the evaluation design process and the questions being explored. That does not mean that the evaluator does not bring their expertise to the conversation. It does mean that there is a discussion about the process and a joint agreement about how community partners will be engaged.

Second, the work of sensemaking is a shared goal between the community and the evaluator. We want to engage in questions that enhance our collective understanding of the community change story we have embarked on together. This commitment requires the evaluator to meet with the community partners at various stages of the evaluation for discussion and learning.

Third, together we answer the questions "So what?" and "Now what?" There is agreement that we discuss the relevance of our findings and that we will jointly agree on the action items identified in the evaluation. This is critical for turning learning into action. When an evaluation helps us to gain a deeper understanding or identify a correction, we can adapt or modify our community plan. If we identify a new direction, we may develop a working group to explore and implement the new idea.

Evaluations Should Seek to Empower, Not Judge

Funders often require evaluations as a form of oversight. The funder would like a neutral third party to verify that the activities and results reported took place. This need causes some evaluators to side with the funder and take on the role of judge. This kind of evaluator seeks to answer the questions and concerns that a funder might have about a project, and is less concerned about the learning needs of the community partners.

Though we want to be deeply respectful and responsive to our funders, it would be wise to discuss reporting needs with them early in our partnership. We could discuss the various kinds of evaluations that advance community change. It is my experience that funders are more receptive to undertaking evaluations as a form of learning. Funder questions and the need for data can often be addressed through comprehensive reporting or incorporated into the scope of the evaluation without being its sole purpose. Evaluations can also be empowering when they take into consideration broader impacts.

Community change work often increases empathy as more and more people learn about social issues. A collaborative that desires to include everyone builds diversity and advances equity, especially when there is a commitment to involving those with lived experiences. Evaluators can also encourage learning and change by valuing and tracking learning. As communities learn more about the issues they are addressing, they are positioned for better outcomes. When they learn to work better together, they are strengthening the community for generations to come.

Evaluations Should Include Measurable Data

Asking, "Is our community better because of our work?" helps us to move toward the breakthrough we are seeking. This question is often answered with qualitative anecdotes but less often through numbers. Stories of change about the people we have helped and how their lives have improved are much more powerful when we also share numerical data that demonstrates that the stories are representative of changes for the whole community.

Population-level change is remarkably difficult to track. Census data is periodic and can take years to become public.

Try to seek other forms of community data that may be more timely. In Canada, tracking tax filer data is often more useful, but again it is difficult to access because of privacy issues and even more difficult to interpret. The very idea of population-level change is motivating for partners in a community change initiative. It is worth the effort to consider various approaches to reporting.

Broadening focus beyond population-level change is important. Achieving change at this level is a multiyear journey and you must have measures that help you understand when you have achieved milestones, so you are celebrating successes on the journey toward population-level impact. This is essential to build and sustain momentum and commitment.

I would suggest that the desire to see population-level data changes is important but should be only one way to determine your success or outcomes. The key is to consider your contribution to the changes you see and learn from the data. It is important to have multiple ways of determining success.

Evaluators Should Be Partners

Evaluators engaged in community change collaboratives or networks can be valuable partners because they bring a unique set of skills and insights that can help the community to break through and achieve better outcomes. Take time to find an evaluator who truly understands community change and the methodologies for evaluating at the community level. Not all evaluators have the skills and patience to work with community partners and stakeholders. It is wise to take the time to find an evaluation partner that can.

For Further Learning

Cabaj, Mark. "Evaluating Collective Impact: Five Simple Rules." *The Philanthropist* 26, no. 1 (2014): 109.

Cabaj, Mark. *Evaluating Systems Change. Results: An Inquiry Framework.* Waterloo, ON: Tamarack Institue, 2019.

Fetterman, David M., Liliana Rodriguez-Campos, and Ann P. Zukoski. *Collaborative, Participatory, and Empowerment Evaluation: Stakeholder Involvement Approaches.* New York: Guilford Press, 2018.

Patton, Michael Quinn. *Developmental Evaluation: Applying Complexity Concepts to Enhance Innovation and Use.* New York: Guilford Press, 2011.

Patton, Michael Quinn. *Utilization-Focused Evaluation.* 5th Edition. Thousand Oaks, CA: Sage, 2021.

Conclusion

Be Careful What You Wish For

Yes, a dandelion
because they are a flower
of wishes. You blow that ball
of seeds and the wind carries them to the one
assigned to grant or reject.
And it's a good thing
that it's the dandelions
who have this power
because they are tough
and sometimes you have to be tough
to even remember
that you have any desires left at all,
to believe that even one
could be satisfied, would not turn
to an example of
"be careful what you wish for,
it might come true."

—FROM "LUCIEN'S BIRTHDAY POEM"
BY ELLIE SCHOENFELD (USED WITH PERMISSION)

WHAT WILL CAUSE YOU TO step forward with others to make things right in your community? What do you wish for? What is causing your hesitancy?

There is a famous YouTube video of a man listening to street musicians. Everyone is standing around, but he feels the need to dance. He gets up and starts dancing. Alone he looks like a fool, swinging his arms and bopping his head while kicking up his feet. He dances alone for some time. Everyone is watching. Then another man stands to join him. They see each other and start to dance with each other. Soon there is a third, and then a fourth, and suddenly the whole audience begins to dance.

Was it the man who started to dance that caused this reaction? Or was it the man who stood up second and joined him, validating the dance? Or was it the third or the fourth person that started to dance, or was it the crowd itself? They wanted to dance, but they just needed someone to start.

I believe that many of the social issues, and the brokenness we see and feel in our communities, are felt by most of us. We see many different people struggle: single parents, alienated families, young people, and those dealing with mental health issues. We see the effects of climate change, poverty, and racism on our neighbors. We are, though, somehow frozen—frozen together like ice cubes that melted just enough to touch each other before they froze again. We want to dance, but we are stuck. Or maybe we are just waiting for a sign or an opportunity to act. And yet, so often we wait, and nothing changes.

In this case, our need for a breakthrough is a need to break out. What is causing us not to act? How might we break out? Will you be the first to dance or the second to join in? Will you get up when the crowd joins in?

The world needs our discontent with the ways things are. If we were content, we would accept the brokenness we see daily in our communities. We would accept the fear our children have of their future and climate change. We would accept the misery of the homeless mother struggling to care for her children, and the fractious and seemingly futile struggle of people faced with racism and the inequity it breeds. We would accept the hunger pangs that are never satisfied, the workers that work for less than they need.

And then your discontent makes you tired. The endless struggle seems to always end the same. Does the brokenness you see make your discontent feel more like burnout? Your hope, once ignited by your discontent, flickers. There are days you feel like the light in you will disappear.

You may be a community leader with a title. Perhaps you are a CEO, executive director, or manager. You may not get paid to do the work of caring. You may be a business owner, construction worker, or musician. You may be a community leader with no title. You may be retired, unemployed, or on sick leave. Your title or lack thereof might make you feel like doing more is not about you. That caring is something that you are, not something that you do.

The ideas and the practices shared in this book come from the thousands of people who have broken out and had a breakthrough. You have read their stories. They are known in my world as the Tamarack Community. The learners who have joined together learn to act together. They have turned their discontent into collective action. They address the root causes of the problems their communities face.

You want more for your community because you care.

Elizabeth had worked all her life to improve conditions in Des Moines, Iowa, and wanted better outcomes for racially affected neighborhoods. Des Moines had just been named the ninth worst place in America for black people to live. She rallied her community and formed Opportunities Central Iowa. Thousands in her community joined the dance.

Carole and Joanne were important leaders in their community. On a trip to Russia, Carol was asked by one of her hosts, "How can you tolerate so much child poverty in a wealthy community like Hamilton?" This fueled her discontent. When she returned home, she ask Joanne to dance with her to change the circumstances for children in their community. Hundreds joined the dance.

Aysha, a nurse, had seen the effects of cancer destroy many lives. She joined the Maine Cancer Foundation to try to change circumstances for Mainers. She rallied her organization and then her entire state and formed a network to reduce the effects of cancer and address some of the root causes. Hundreds, including many cancer survivors, joined in the dance.

Each of these community leaders broke out of their discontent and worked to achieve a breakthrough for their communities. They did this by bringing diverse people into a form of common agenda. By uniting diverse leaders—including those with lived experience—in a dance for change, they enabled a common agenda that changed everything.

I hope that this book will be your guide for many years to come. That you will use it to fuel and guide that which you wish for yourself and your community. That this book will help you and your community write your own book about your discontent, and the dance you undertook to turn that discontent into a common agenda that changed everything.

I hope that you will break out and achieve your breakthrough.

I hope that what you wish for just might come true.

Breakthrough Community Change
Discussion Guide

Breakthrough community change happens when people connect to learn, discuss, and agree on a future they want to build
together with their community. This book is written as a guide
and can be used to facilitate learning and agreement. The
questions below can be addressed by an individual, groups,
and organizations, and during community conversations.

INDIVIDUAL REFLECTION

- What are your personal motivations for seeking a
  breakthrough community change?
- What is the change you want to see in your community?
- What are the five "root causes" of the issue you want to
  change?
- Can you name five assets your community has to
  address these root causes?
- How do you currently think community change occurs?
  (Your theory of change)
- Who in your community would you like to learn
  together with about this work?

GROUP DISCUSSION

- What does community mean to you?
- What does collaborating mean to you?
- What does "communities collaborating" mean to you?

- What is the community change you each want to see?
- What is the value of seeking a breakthrough community change?

ORGANIZATIONAL STAFF DISCUSSION

- What is the community issue that requires better outcomes?
- How would the better outcomes you seek serve your clients?
- What are the systemic barriers facing your clients?
- What assets/skills/talents/resources are available in your organization?
- How could a common community agenda change everything for your clients?
- What assets are you willing to share for a breakthrough community change campaign?

COMMUNITY CONVERSATIONS

Consider bringing a diverse group of people together from your community and host a conversation. This can be a starting point to building broader engagement and begin the change you want to see.

- Who am I and why is it important I am here today?
- What is happening in our community now that needs change?
- What is the community change I want to see and how will this make a difference?
- What would a community change breakthrough mean to me?
- How might a common agenda change everything?

Notes

Introduction

1   *https://www.statcan.gc.ca/en/topics-start/poverty.*

Chapter 2

1   Maine's Impact Cancer Network, Maine Cancer Foundation, and Maine CDC Comprehensive Cancer Control Program, *Maine Cancer Plan 2021–2025*, ed. Patricia Hart (Augusta: Maine Center for Disease Control and Prevention, 2021).

2   Deloitte and the Business Community Anti-Poverty Initiative, *Organizational Review and Future Directions* (Saint John, New Brunswick: Business Community Anti-Poverty Initiative, 2021), *https://www.bcapi.ca/s/Final-Report-BCAPI-Recommendations-and-Future-Direction-2021-03.pdf.*

Chapter 4

1   Henry Mintzberg, "The Fall and Rise of Strategic Planning," *Harvard Business Review* (January–February 1994), *https://hbr.org/1994/01/the-fall-and-rise-of-strategic-planning.*

2   David Bohm and Lee Nichol, *On Dialogue* (London: Routledge, 2004).

Chapter 7

1   Frances Westley, Brenda Zimmerman, and Michael Quinn Patton, *Getting to Maybe: How the World Is Changed* (Toronto: Random House Canada, 2006).

Chapter 8

1   Mark Cabaj, "Evaluating Collective Impact: Five Simple Rules," *The Philanthropist* 26, no. 1 (2014): 109.

2   Cabaj, "Evaluating Collective Impact," 109.

3   John Kania and Mark Kramer, "Collective Impact," *Stanford Social Innovation Review* 9, no. 1 (Winter 2011): 36–41.

Chapter 10

1   David Brooks, "Winning the War on Poverty: The Canadians Are Doing It; We're Not," *New York Times*, April 4, 2019, *https://www .nytimes.com/2019/04/04/opinion/canada-poverty-record.html*.

Chapter 11

1   Paul Born, *Leaderful Communities: A Study in Community Leadership* (Saarbrücken, Germany: VDM Verlag, 2008).

Chapter 13

1   John Kania and Mark Kramer, "Collective Impact," *Stanford Social Innovation Review* 9, no. 1 (Winter 2011): 36–41.

2   ORS Impact and Spark Policy Institute, *When Collective Impact Has an Impact: A Cross-Site Study of 25 Collective Impact Initiatives* (Seattle and Denver: ORS Impact and Spark Policy Institute, 2018).

3   Ibid.

4   Liz Weaver and Mark Cabaj, *Collective Impact 3.0: An Evolving Framework for Community Change* (Waterloo, ON: Tamarack Institute, 2016).

5   Ibid.

Chapter 14

1   Megan Courtney, Liz Weaver, and Sylvia Cheuy, *Reflections on Community Change: Two Countries, Two Perspectives, One Vision Moving Forward* (Wellington, NZ and Waterloo, ON: Inspiring Communities and Tamarack Institute, 2018).

2   Jason Mogus and Tom Lucas, *Networked Change: How Progressive Campaigns Are Won in the 21st Century* (Salt Spring Island, BC: NetChange Consulting, 2016).

3   Alison Homer, *Engaging People with Lived/Living Experience: A Guide for Including People in Poverty Reduction* (Waterloo, ON: Tamarack Institute, 2020).

Chapter 15

1   Al Etmanski, *Impact: Six Patterns to Spread Your Social Innovation* (Vancouver, BC: Orwell Cove, 2015).

2   Frances Westley, Brenda Zimmerman, and Michael Quinn Patton, *Getting to Maybe: How the World Is Changed* (Toronto: Random House Canada, 2006).

Chapter 16

1   Megan Courtney, Liz Weaver, and Sylvia Cheuy, *Reflections on Community Change: Two Countries, Two Perspectives, One Vision Moving Forward* (Wellington, NZ and Waterloo, ON: Inspiring Communities and Tamarack Institute, 2018).

2   David Chrislip and Carl Larson, *Collaborative Leadership: How Citizens and Civic Leaders Can Make a Difference* (San Francisco: Jossey-Bass, 1994).

Chapter 17

1   Michael Quinn Patton, *Utilization-Focused Evaluation*, 5th Edition (Thousand Oaks, CA: Sage, 2021).

2   David M. Fetterman and Abraham Wandersman, eds., *Empowerment Evaluation Principles in Practice* (New York: Guilford Press, 2005); David M. Fetterman and Abraham Wandersman, "Empowerment Evaluation: Yesterday, Today, and Tomorrow," *American Journal of Evaluation* 28, no. 2 (2007): 179–98.

With Thanks

To write a book about community truly takes a community.

First, I want to thank Cyndy Wasko, who has spent endless hours supporting me in editing and rewriting this book. I met Cyndy while on a coaching assignment in the San Francisco area, where she hired me to support two community collaborating initiatives. The first was to bring priority of the arts to education, and the second was to advance STEM education for underrepresented people in health professions. Cyndy knows the work of communities collaborating and brings an important thinking system to large-scale change. She is also an exceptional editing partner. Huge thanks, Cyndy.

I also want to thank editor Steve Piersanti and the amazing Berrett-Koehler team for believing in me and this book. This is no ordinary publishing company.

I have dedicated this book to the Tamarack Community. I cofounded the Tamarack Institute with Alan Broadbent of Maytree and the Avana Capital corporation twenty years ago. Working with an amazing team, we have built a community of more than forty-two thousand learners and have active partnerships in more than five hundred cities in Canada, the United States, and around the world. This book is dedicated to the amazing volunteers and staff that have given endless hours, believing that large-scale change for a better world is possible. This book is also dedicated to the learners, the doers, and the community leaders who have given their stories and ideas to the Tamarack Community so this learning could be spread around the globe.

I am deeply grateful to Alan Broadbent, Mark Cabaj, Liz Weaver, Shauna Sylvester, Brock Carlton, Tim Brodhead, Katherine Pearson, Stephen Huddart, Vali Bennett, Colin Robertson, John McKnight, Sherri Torjman, Harold Dueck, Lori Hewson, and Bill Young for the significant contribution that they have made and the thought leadership they have shown in the founding and growing of the institute.

I am specifically grateful to the staff and key thought leaders of the Tamarack Community for reading the draft manuscript of this book and providing the most important feedback and corrections. Thank you, Danya Pastuszek, Liz Weaver, Mark Cabaj, Lyse Brunet, Dilys Tan, Lisa Attygalle, Sylvia Cheuy, Alison Homer, Laura Schnurr, Natasha Pie, and Jill Zacharias.

Writing a book requires many hours of focus and inspiration. I am forever grateful to my family, Marlene, Lucas, Michael, Betty, and Laura, for bringing so much joy, calm, and hope into my life. And to our extended families and a circle of friends that prove the power of community every day.

Wishing everyone much joy!

Index

About the Author

 I came to the work of large-scale impact through my discontent with the results of the community change work I had dedicated my life to. My midlife crisis was wrestling with the questions, "How could the United Nations declare our organization one of the forty best practices in the world while poverty has actually increased in our community? How can you be the best at what you do and still things get worse?"

This midlife crisis resulted in me cofounding the Tamarack Institute. For the next twenty years as the CEO/co-CEO, with the help of my team, Tamarack grew into a learning community of over forty-two thousand active participants in Canada, the United States, and from around the world exploring questions of community change. At the same time, I cofounded and was the CEO of Vibrant Communities, a national network that grew to nearly five hundred cities and communities leading campaigns ending poverty, deepening community, building youth futures, and advancing climate transitions.

The two organizations represented my obsessive need to marry theory with practice. The Tamarack Institute thought about and taught the ideas of community change, while Vibrant Communities would test and apply these ideas to communities. Though seemingly ideal, this combination was not perfect. When learners would ask me, "Are you sure about that?" I would break into a big smile and share, "I am pretty sure we know this works in practice, but I am not yet sure if it works in theory."

I love everything community and have written five books about the possibilities of community thinking and action to build a better world. Two of my books, *Deepening Community* and *Community Conversations*, have gone on to become national best sellers.

My passion is to help people learn about community change. I do this as a coach, often journeying for up to a year with communities embarking on collective impact or communities collaborating campaigns. I love to facilitate community conversations, especially gatherings where organizations or collaboratives bring together diverse groups of people to address challenging issues. Teaching, writing, and giving keynotes are opportunities for me to engage with people all over the world.

As a global faculty member (steward) of the Asset-Based Community Development Institute (ABCD) and as a senior fellow of Ashoka, the world's largest network of social innovators, I have been influenced by a huge network of people made up of some of the best community change leaders in the world. It was a great honor for me when, in 2019, I was appointed to the Order of Canada, Canada's highest civilian honor in recognition of "contributions to his community and for his large-scale initiatives to reduce poverty."

Learn more about me and my work at *PaulBorn.ca* or email me at *pauldborn@gmail.com*.

—*Paul Born C.M.*

Dear reader,

Thank you for picking up this book and welcome to the worldwide BK community! You're joining a special group of people who have come together to create positive change in their lives, organizations, and communities.

What's BK all about?

Our mission is to connect people and ideas to create a world that works for all.

Why? Our communities, organizations, and lives get bogged down by old paradigms of self-interest, exclusion, hierarchy, and privilege. But we believe that can change. That's why we seek the leading experts on these challenges—and share their actionable ideas with you.

A welcome gift

To help you get started, we'd like to offer you a **free copy** of one of our bestselling ebooks:

www.bkconnection.com/welcome

When you claim your **free ebook**, you'll also be subscribed to our blog.

Our freshest insights

Access the best new tools and ideas for leaders at all levels on our blog at ideas.bkconnection.com.

Sincerely,

Your friends at Berrett-Koehler